About the author:

VIVIENNE ANGUS has been a pet owner since the age of four, when she acquired a dog called Blackie, to be followed by a cat called Whiskey. Throughout her adult life cats have been her constant companions, helping her, with her son Matthew, through many painful episodes. She has bred Burmese and runs a small cattery, and more recently she has become a pet counsellor, helping owners with worries about their pets' welfare or in times of bereavement. Her articles have been published in the *Journal of the Society for Companion Animal Studies*, *Cat World* and *Veterinary Practice*, and she has broadcast on radio and television on the relationship between cats and owners. She and her son live in Devon, where she is at present working on her second book.

Know Yourself Through Your Cat

Vivienne Angus

New York London Toronto Sydney Tokyo Singapore

First published in Great Britain by
Souvenir Press Ltd, 1991
First published in Great Britain by Pocket Books, 1993
An imprint of Simon & Schuster Ltd
A Paramount Communications Company

Simon & Schuster Ltd
West Garden Place
Kendal Street
London W2 2AQ

Simon & Schuster of Australia Pty Ltd
Sydney

A CIP catalogue record for this book is
available from the British Library
ISBN 0-671-85072-5

Typeset in Sabon 10/11.5 by
Hewer Text Composition Services, Edinburgh
Printed and bound in Great Britain by
HarperCollins Manufacturing, Glasgow

For Yasmin:
simply, 'Thank you.'

Acknowledgements

Thank you to all my friends, human and feline, for their patience, help and support – not forgetting my son Matthew.

Thank you also to Harley Swiftdeer Reagan for the information on native American Indian culture.

Finally, I should like to thank Stuart Wilson for his invaluable help and encouragement, Wendy Newman for her delightful drawings, and Kate Mount for her beautiful photographs.

I am grateful to the following for permission to quote from copyright material: J. G. Ferguson Publishing Company for passages by Aniela Jaffé from *Man and his Symbols*, edited by C. G. Jung; Methuen London for material from *Incredible Cats* by David Greene; the British Small Animal Veterinary Association for a quotation from *Manual of Canine Behaviour* by Valerie O'Farrell (BSAVA Publication 1986); Random House

Inc. and Collins for an extract from *Memories, Dreams, Reflections* by C. G. Jung, translated by Richard and Clara Winston, edited by Aniela Jaffé. Passages from *Cat Talk: What Your Cat is Trying to Tell You* by Carole C. Wilbourn (Copyright © 1979 by Carole C. Wilbourn) are reprinted with permission of Macmillan Publishing Company.

Despite every effort being made, it has proved impossible to trace the copyright holders of *The Outermost House* by Henry Beeston, from which I have quoted in Chapter 5. I regret that I have therefore been unable to obtain the appropriate permission. Due acknowledgement will willingly be made in any future printing should the copyright holder be found.

Contents

Introduction

Some time ago I went through a very unhappy phase in my life. My whole outlook became dominated by feelings of fear and pain, and at last I decided to undertake a course of Jungian therapy. Little did I know that I was embarking on a voyage of discovery, not only of my own mind, but also of my relationship with my cats, which was to lead me to a greater understanding of myself and them. I had always identified strongly with my cats, so it seemed only natural that much of my therapy should involve examining the way I related to them, since this revealed much about myself of which I had been unaware.

Why we share our lives with cats, and how we treat them, is a fascinating subject, and in this book I have attempted to explore the many reasons why we become so involved with them.

If you are close to your cats you may not have realised what a valuable asset this can be in the process of self-understanding. By studying your cats and using them as a mirror to reveal aspects of yourself and your unconscious choices, you can develop your own self-awareness. Although the path to self-understanding is a long one, I believe it can lead to a peace of mind which is rare in this world of fear, tension and anxiety. Indeed, throughout the ages it has been advocated by many religious and esoteric philosophies as a route to tranquillity and spiritual enlightenment.

This book is based partly on the psychology of Carl Jung and partly on my own knowledge and experience of keeping and studying cats over a period of thirty years. I have passed on what I learnt in my search for self-understanding so that you, the reader, can also learn about your own nature through examining your relationship with your cats and the reasons for your mutual attraction. You will find that some words are used not in their general or popular sense, so I have included a short glossary at the end of the book to help clarify them. I have also added a list of books on Jung and on cat behaviour, which you may find useful.

We are only just beginning to understand how great a part Jungian psychology may be able to play in the quest for self-knowledge and inner growth. In the future the value of his perception of the human condition may be much more widely appreciated, and the application of his methods may lead to an expansion of self-awareness. Through this process our cat companions will also benefit, because we should then be better able to give them the care and respect they deserve.

1

What Attracts You to Your Cat?

Mirror, mirror on the wall, am I the most perfect cat of all?
Have you ever wondered exactly what it is that attracts
you to your cat, and why you prefer one kind of cat to
another? Choosing a cat is not so arbitrary as it might
seem – in fact you will find that there are a number of
basic principles which underlie this process.

'Doesn't Aunt Maud look like her dog!' exclaims your
nine-year-old.

'Don't be silly, dear,' you reply – until you take a look
for yourself, and realise that your child was being very
perceptive. Aunt Maud *does* look like her dog! This is not
just coincidence, it is all part of the process of projection,
and although with cats there is less diversity in body shape
and colour than you find in dog breeds, the same general
principle of projection applies.

All cats evoke feelings in us. From the sweet little
kitten, through the whole spectrum of felines to the

powerful panther, each one strikes an emotional chord. The kitten appeals to the child within us, playful and vulnerable, while in contrast the awesome strength of the panther reminds us of our potential unleashed power. We identify with, and recognise, something of ourselves in these animals.

This principle applies not only to cats: all animals are symbolic to us. We feel attracted to and project onto those animals which evoke in us feelings that are close to our own personality; they symbolise a part of ourselves. For the same reason we can also be afraid of some animals: they may represent a part of ourselves which we cannot come to terms with or accept. This process takes place in our unconscious and is happening continually in all aspects of our lives. Once projection has occurred we become emotionally entangled, but by looking at the object of our projection and what we feel for it (positive or negative), we can be helped to understand ourselves.

All cats exude a sense of power and self-containment, but they also represent the unconscious, the feminine, the introverted side of our minds, and that is why I have found my relationship with them so interesting.

We project onto our cats and they fulfil various roles – as companions, and occasionally as substitutes for human relationships or for our own children. But apart from the rare exception, I think that the average person who keeps and enjoys animals as companions is not substituting them for relationships with people, but rather *supplementing* their human relationships, because animals help us to relate to the aspects of ourselves which they symbolise.

I became particularly aware of this rapport on one occasion when I had a visit from the six-year-old daughter of a friend of mine. She arrived at the door bubbling with eagerness.

'Could Imelda see William?' her mother asked, adding, 'she's been pestering me for ages to come and see him again.'

William, my red point Siamese, was in the lounge, reclining on a rug in the sunshine and looking very aristocratic. Imelda went to him and made a fuss of him, and I asked her why it was William and not the other cats that she had particularly wanted to see again.

'It's his crossed eyes,' she replied. 'I can make my eyes go crossed, too – ' she demonstrated this. 'And he has blue eyes, just like me.' She was very aware that she liked William because he resembled her more closely than did the other two cats. In fact Imelda and William also have similar hair colour and both are slim and elegant, so it is not surprising that she identified with him.

I saw the same process at work when my friend Caryll first made William's acquaintance. Caryll is very attractive, with long golden hair and clear, aquiline features in the classic mould. She is a well-balanced person, with a friendly, caring nature, and has always been greatly interested in understanding her spiritual side. She is naturally attracted to cats, and when she originally decided to get one her preference was for a male. In this case, however, the whole family was involved in the choice, and the cat they finally opted for was a female tabby, which had led a semi-wild life on a local farm. They named her Missy.

Caryll projected very strongly onto Missy, but because the little cat had had a fairly negative start she was unable to fulfil Caryll's desire for a very close companion. She tried to the best of her ability, and Caryll helped her, doing much to increase her confidence. Missy learnt to communicate with Caryll when she was unwell, and was as affectionate as she could allow herself to be; but although Caryll loved her very much, she still felt the need for an even closer relationship with a cat. Her unconscious was exerting a strong pull.

Hearing that I owned two cats – William, the red point Siamese, and a female chocolate Burmese called Hooli – she asked if she could come to see them. She had heard that they were very affectionate and was clearly excited about meeting them as she walked in with her husband, Kit. On going into the lounge her glance fell on Hooli, and she immediately bent down to stroke her. William, meanwhile, whom she had not yet noticed, was sitting above her on a nearby table, sniffing her hair. When Kit told her to look up quickly, she came nose to nose with William.

Her reaction was immediate. Here sat her perfect image of Cat, a golden-blond creature (William is a soft peach colour) with aquiline features, piercing blue eyes and a perfect air of mystery and omniscience. It was love at first sight! The impression was so strong that even now, after visiting a local cat show with some five hundred entries of many breeds, it is still a male red point Siamese that Caryll desires.

Different shapes of cat attract different people. Whereas

an oriental cat may seem the most beautiful to a person with aquiline features like Caryll, someone with a rounded face may find long-haired breeds more appealing. There may also be a physical resemblance in terms of colour, as there is for Imelda and Caryll, linking you with your cat. For example, if you have blue-grey hair, then perhaps a blue point cat will seem the most attractive to you.

Many other factors dictate our choice where colour and coat pattern are concerned, some of them based on ingrained preconceptions. We tend to regard all cats of a particular colour and pattern as having the same sort of character – for instance, we often associate ginger cats with aggressiveness. This may be because, with their reddish coloration, they seem to radiate energy and pugnacity – after all, we view the colour red as symbolic of energy, and people with red hair are often assumed to have hot tempers. There is also a common belief that all ginger cats are male, and this could add to the myth that they are more aggressive than other cats; male cats, especially entire males, need to defend a larger territory and to fight for the favours of females. 'The ginger tom from next door' is almost a byword.

Ginger cats can of course be male or female, although males are more common, and they are no more aggressive than cats of any other colour. I have known ginger cats of a most sweet and gentle disposition – although I have also encountered several which fully lived up to their fiery reputation.

One in particular made life for two cats of mine very unpleasant. My first two Siamese, Tangi, a male seal point, and Mieling, a chocolate point female, lived with me in a small bungalow. The garden, although not large, was well stocked with shrubs, one large tree, a lawn and various cat toys. Next door lived a large neutered ginger tom named Ginger, and his garden was totally bare. He would watch with envy as Tangi and Mieling played with their carpet-tunnels and tea-chests and climbed their tree. He made frequent attempts to take over their garden as his territory, and many a battle with Tangi ensued.

When I was going out I would shut Tangi and Mieling indoors. This was Ginger's cue: he would climb over the chain-link fence and play on their toys, while they watched helplessly from the window, their whiskers bristling in fury. And to make matters worse he would leer at them as he strutted about on their toys. Ginger's lack of playthings must have been discussed in his own home, because one day the man of the house arrived back with a tree. He marched into the garden with a certain amount of aggression (which, one only supposes, must have been the result of being nagged by Ginger's mistress), dug a pit, shoved in the tree, filled it in and marched indoors. The entire scenario was observed by Ginger, who was looking duly proud, and by Tangi and Mieling from their own side of the fence. Ginger then proceeded to climb his new tree with an extremely smug expression, but as the tree had not been properly supported it wobbled and bent over, with Ginger clinging grimly to it. After picking himself up and removing the mud from his fur, he noticed Tangi and Mieling next door, laughing behind their paws. Ginger walked towards them, slapped their faces through the fence, and stalked away with as much dignity as he could muster.

The feud continued for a long time, with Ginger living up to his archetypal personality. Finally Tangi and Mieling had had enough, and they apparently used their Siamese intelligence to devise a plan that would put him in his place once and for all. I watched from the house as they hid amongst the vegetables at a place where they knew Ginger would enter the garden, and when he climbed the fence and landed in the vegetable patch, they both pounced on him. All I saw was a whirling ball as the three of them rolled over and over, and as soon as Ginger managed to free himself he made off, never to bother them to the same extent again.

Tortoiseshell cats, in contrast to ginger, are predominantly female; very rarely, however, a male tortoiseshell may be born and usually these males are sterile. The image of a tortoiseshell is of a gentle cat – again, I do not know how much of this is fact and how much fiction, but being predominantly female may be the reason this concept came about. All the tortoiseshell cats I have known have been gentle animals, but I have heard stories to the contrary.

A cat's coat pattern and colour may influence our perception of its character, but this perception can be built up from symbols which incorporate these factors, along with projection, myths, superstition and experience of other cats. Even if there is a similarity in the character of cats of the same colour, a cat's personality can be enhanced or modified by early experiences: an extrovert ginger may be inhibited, and a loving blue have its nervous tendency emphasised, through ill treatment. Therefore in Chapter 2, where I have grouped each colour or coat pattern according to similarities in character, I have based it on what these colours and patterns might generally symbolise to us.

Type and breed form my main groupings in Chapter 3, for these also affect our choice and perceptions, but another important factor is the choice of a male or a female (see the section on the general unconscious in Chapter 4).

If you are attracted to several different colours and breeds, this simply means that all these represent different aspects of you, and whichever is the most dominant at the time will be the main element in influencing your decision. But there are also influences operating at a much deeper emotional level, and these too may affect your choice. You may choose your cat because it aligns with a particular need that you have at that time. If, for instance, you see a cat which is unwanted, or in pain or distress, you may project onto it if you yourself are unhappy. Projection is seeing something of yourself in others, so these strong emotions may overwhelm any other projections of colour and character. As your love is given to the cat in an attempt to ease its pain, it then returns that love to you, and together you help each other. Another example of the emotional aspect being the strongest projection is the need to nurture, and often the weak one in a litter of kittens will be chosen first as a result of this. But once you are aware of your actions and have acquired a little more self-understanding, your decision to look after the helpless little kitten may not be based entirely on unconscious desires, but partly on a conscious choice to love and care for a creature in need.

Sometimes you might choose a kitten because it is the quietest or the naughtiest; these decisions again are projections and reflect your own character and circumstances. You might choose a quiet kitten if you are so busy and preoccupied that you prefer an undemanding animal, or the kitten might balance your personality by representing an aspect of yourself that is not predominant. On the other hand, it might be a straightforward projection of your rather shy, conservative personality. A naughty kitten might reflect your own rebellious nature, self-confidence, individualism or sense of humour. You might choose it if you feel all these things about yourself but do not have the confidence to behave that way. It is not difficult to examine the reasons why you personally choose one type of cat rather than another, and it can be quite informative about your own character. Occasionally you simply cannot make up your mind when faced with a bundle of kittens, but then something seems to 'tell' you which one to have. Your unconscious knows which one you want or need, even if you yourself are not aware of it. That is, of course, if the kitten doesn't choose you first. They seem to have an uncanny knack of knowing what will suit them.

When I had kittens to home I was always interested in people's choices. I particularly remember Graham, whom I met when he answered an advertisement for

one of Hooli's kittens. I had been very protective of the
kittens, and very particular about the people they should
live with; I felt I had engineered their birth and it was
therefore my responsibility to find them caring homes. I
had four kittens left out of the seven, and had decided that
if I did not feel right about their prospective new homes I
would keep them all myself. One last advertisement was
planned, and if that failed my cat family would stay at six
instead of two or three as I had intended.

Graham turned up in answer to this advertisement,
accompanied by his girl-friend Jenni and her daughter
Harriet. Despite Jenni's feeling that he should not have
a cat because he was away at work all day, Graham was
certain he wanted one. He had been thinking about it for
a year, ever since he had moved into his new home, so the
decision had not been taken lightly. He was in his early
thirties, appeared quiet and gentle, and I felt at ease with
him. He explained that he was a school teacher, and that
his subject was sport. Realising that he would be out much
of the time, I advised him to have two kittens rather than
one. One kitten on its own would have been desperately
unhappy if left alone for long periods, after coming from
a home full of cats; and Burmese, being very bright, get
bored quickly if they have little stimulus. After giving it
some thought he agreed that this was the right decision,
and the choosing of the kittens began.

I had three chocolate females and one lilac female. I
had thought I might keep the lilac for myself, but because
Graham had agreed to have two kittens I said he could
have the choice of any of them. The first one he chose

was Tinkerbell, a very pretty chocolate, not as naughty as her sister Minky or as Siamese-looking as Gretel. I think, left to himself, he might have chosen Minky as the second kitten, but Jenni and Harriet liked lilac Jewel. She had a very sweet, gentle personality, and Graham agreed to take her.

Some time later I visited Graham to see how he was getting on. The kittens had taken him over, and he was fascinated with them. I asked him which was his favourite. Tinkerbell was the one he thought most attractive, but he preferred Jewel's personality. I think this was because the lilac, with her very obviously feminine image, was difficult for him to accept, but his unconscious did not have this handicap, and his gentle, quiet, kind attributes were being projected onto Jewel. Yet Tinkerbell, presenting the less feminine image of the two, was more acceptable to his conscious male image.

So, although you may be unaware of it, the cat's colour, coat pattern, breed, character, the situation you find it in, and your own emotional needs, will all be influencing your decision and matching you to your cat.

Elinor is a classic example of the way this process works. She is a very caring woman, who has devoted a considerable amount of her time to self-understanding; an intuitive person with a great respect for the cat world. When I first knew her she had been happily married for six years, with a daughter, Kate, aged four, and a son just nine months old. Although she enjoyed the companionship of cats, she had been put off by several attempts to keep one, all of which had ended unhappily. Driven by Kate's enthusiasm, however, she agreed that they should have just one more try.

She chose Peanuts, a long-haired ginger female – the ginger colour indicating energy and adventure, and the female element showing that this energy was not being used to the full because of her commitment to a domestic situation. Peanuts thrived and grew into a magnificent cat, but always attached herself more to Elinor than to any other member of the family. At that time Elinor's life was full: looking after two young children kept her busy, and Peanuts' temperament fitted the situation perfectly. She proved an extremely adaptable cat, taking house-moves in her stride; and yet, true to her ginger character, she was

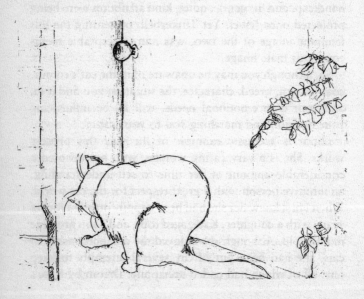

not a cat to be tampered with. Everyone had to know their place as far as Peanuts was concerned, and if you stepped over the mark you would soon know it. But as long as that was understood, Peanuts assumed the position of a cat which observed life with a tolerant understanding; and provided you knew the rules she had a very amiable nature.

Five years later found Elinor divorced and moved into her own house. Peanuts took the move in her usual adaptable way, but in the new house she grew restless and clearly needed company, so it was just as well that a new cat was about to arrive on the scene. Elinor had heard of a tortie point Siamese named Isis who was very unhappy in her home, spending most of her time on top of a table, avoiding other animal members of the household. The attraction to Isis was instant, and Elinor felt a strong bond with her which was to last and grow throughout the cat's life. Perhaps Elinor was relating to Isis' distress: feeling lost and in a difficult situation was an experience common to both of them at this time in their lives. Isis quickly settled down with Elinor, but objected to the presence of Peanuts whom she obviously saw as a threat to her happy new family. However, after a week Isis had begun to accept Peanuts, and they became good friends, enjoying and benefiting from each other's company. For two years Isis lived a very happy life. Unfortunately she then became ill and nothing could be done to save her. Her loss was felt by the whole family and their friends: she had been such a bright cat, with a delightful nature.

By now Elinor had met Robert, and although he was

to become an important and happy part of her life, at this point she still had a lot of trauma in the background, and a lot of problems to be worked through. Feeling trapped by her circumstances, it was no surprise that the next cat in her life proved to be quite different. I had told her about Myrtle, a pretty little seal point Siamese, who lived with her owner in a hairdressing salon. Myrtle had never felt really settled, since her owner was always too busy to give her all the attention she needed. She was left to wander amongst the customers, moving from one lap to another. This left her without a sense of belonging, unable to find her own secure niche. The owner, wisely recognising this, looked for a new home for Myrtle, and again it was love at first sight. The cat fitted perfectly into Elinor's life because she, too, was just then looking for a new niche for herself.

Once at home with Elinor, Myrtle was allowed to find herself. For the first time in her life she experienced some freedom, and she was even allowed a litter of kittens before being neutered. Myrtle blossomed, and so did Elinor. Robert moved in, and life for Elinor began anew, just around the time when Myrtle had her kittens. There were four of them, the first-born being a breech-birth that required Elinor's help: a large male kitten. In consequence, a very strong bond was formed between Elinor, Myrtle and Shere Khan, as the kitten was named. Elinor had an overwhelming desire to keep this kitten, not just because she had helped him into the world, but because he was male. Unconsciously she was bringing in her male element, and it felt right to be balancing this energy at this point in her life. Up to now she had chosen only female cats.

And what a male Shere Khan turned out to be! Right from the beginning he was the biggest and brightest kitten. Pure black and half Siamese, he had arrogance and elegance all rolled into one – a magnificent cat, and he knew it. Elinor found him captivating; he represented her male energy, which in her search for self-understanding she was now beginning to accept, although at the time she did not consciously recognise this. Shere Khan grew too big for his boots, feeling secure in his environment, but after a few battles he and Myrtle achieved a balance. Elinor's life is now very happy and settled, and Peanuts watches it all with her usual adaptable and tolerant nature.

2

Choosing Your Cat by Colour and Coat Pattern

In order to interpret yourself through your cat according to its colour, coat pattern, type and breed, all you have to do is take the most predominant colour or coat pattern (described below) and combine it with the type and breed of cat (described in Chapter 3). If you own a cat with coloured points, then the colour of its points is the colour to select. For example, if your cat is a lilac point Siamese, read the sections on both lilac cats and oriental cats. Apart from black and white cats, the same principle of selecting the predominant colour applies to bicoloured, tipped or shaded cats – although if there is a lot of white on the cat it does seem to reduce the effect of the colour or coat pattern on its character, so that a ginger and white cat may have a more modified form of the ginger personality.

What this analysis eventually leads to is a whole new way of looking at yourself, using your cat as the key to reveal fresh aspects of your personality. See how much of yourself you can recognise by studying your cat in this way. But remember, this only applies if your cat is the result of a free choice on your part; if the cat was 'inherited' with the house, or was chosen by another member of your family, then you have not been able to exercise a free choice. However, even in cases like these, it is still possible to gain an insight into your personality by referring to the section dealing with the kind of cat which you find most visually and emotionally attractive. And of course you can also study your personality through looking at the way you treat your cat (see Chapter 5).

THE CAT: *Ginger and Cream, including Red Tabby*

Represents the male principle, and energy

He appears to be a very masculine cat, a direct, self-willed cat who seems to know his own mind; he likes to be noticed and makes a great companion because of his strong will and sense of humour. He also seems to have a taste for adventure. Even if he is of a more gentle disposition he will still have something definite to say about life. When a ginger cat is affectionate he may carry it to extremes – after all, ginger reflects energy and that can be channelled into aggression or affection. The image of a fit and healthy ginger cat is vitality, energy and independence.

THE CAT: *Tortoiseshell Pattern and Tri-coloureds (Black, Red and White)*

Represents the female principle

As the tortoiseshell cat is predominantly female, her character is opposite to ginger. She does not hold the feminine mystery like a black cat, but rather expresses the more obvious feminine traits. The tri-coloured cat is considered the good-luck colour in Japan, whilst in a Scottish home a tortoiseshell cat is thought to bring health. She is a cat with a maternal quality, pretty and decorative, appearing to watch life quietly go by, but not averse to some fun and mischief if given the opportunity. After all, she also has some red in her coat! She appears to be a bright, affectionate cat, quite unassuming and with a charming innocence.

THE CAT: *Grey and Brown Tabby Pattern*

The universal cat, represents art

All domestic cats evolved from the tabby. Even in self-coloured cats you can still see faint tabby markings, and as all cats are basically tabby even the most selective breeding can only mask the markings, not eliminate them. The mackerel – tiger striped – tabby is the true wild type marking, rather than the blotched ('classic') pattern.

The tabby gives the impression of always being there, a part of the family. Perhaps this is because in our inherited memory we have known the tabby longer than any other

colour of cat. A beautiful cat, its coat pattern is very
artistic, wild and individual, and perhaps this is the key
word for tabby, *individual*: cats of this colour and pattern
can vary widely in character. Its individuality is typical as
it seems to encompass all cats' characteristics. It is also an
adaptable cat, one you feel you can trust, but it still main-
tains its air of independence. Nevertheless this is a very
open and relaxing cat, with a comfortable feeling about it.

THE CAT: Grey or Blue

Represents dignity

A noble, individualistic and sophisticated cat, and one
who knows it. It is usually intelligent but appears to

Tabby and white cat

be a bit snobbish and very busy doing its own thing. The grey cat gives the impression of a cool, calm character, but I feel this can hide a nervousness, and it is happiest in a steady home. Grey has a detached, dignified feeling and the independent air of this cat can make it appear self-assured. Grey cats are not very common and are often sought by people wishing to have a more unusual colour. It can be very affectionate and gentle on its own terms and this gives us the feeling of being honoured by its attention, which indeed we are.

THE CAT: Black

Represents the mystery of the unconscious

This cat symbolises the feminine mystique. It is a very beautiful and spiritual cat, full of mystery, and because of this it is the cat most persecuted by unthinking people. Never predictable, full of mischief, it is an intelligent, energetic cat, appearing to possess a great deal of wisdom, which is locked away and not always shared. If it is shared, then this happens only under special circumstances such as when you feel at one with this cat. Black cats seem able to read and understand our thoughts; it may be that their eyes, glowing in amongst their black fur, appear to penetrate our minds and reflect our own image. One feels in awe of the black cat; it epitomises Cat, the untamed and unfathomable.

THE CAT: Black and White

Represents harmony and balance

Black and white symbolise good and bad, light and darkness, Yang and Yin, heaven and earth, and the personalities of black and white cats appear to reflect this. Owners seem to think black and white cats can be as good as gold or very naughty. I don't think they are any different from other cats in this respect, but their colour may be influencing people's image of them. Some people find this the clown of the cat world, because of all the cartoon characters it represents. A clean black and white cat has a well-dressed appearance, giving the impression it knows a lot about life and could tell you a thing or two, but because it is a cat you always feel it would keep some things secret. Because of its solid, balanced air, it makes a good listener. I am told that black and white cats have a keen sense of humour if their owners take the time to encourage this by playing games with them.

THE CAT: White

Represents order

The opposite end of the spectrum from black. A well-groomed white cat has a meticulous and tidy quality about it, a beautiful cat with a gentle feeling. It does not appear to hold the sense of wildness that cats of other colours have, hence people may feel more comfortable with it if they have a particular problem relating to this aspect of cats. Innocent-looking, with sometimes a trace of arrogance and disdain, white cats do seem to frighten some people who feel they have a ghostly appearance. They may sometimes appear rather distant, and this could be because some white cats have a problem with deafness. Breeders of white cats are making an effort to breed the fault out of their lines.

On the whole the white cat is a peaceful, gentle cat with a delicate and dainty image.

THE CAT: Brown or Chocolate

Represents well-being and comfort

Plain brown is not a colour found in ordinary cats, but is common in pedigree cats. It is a comfortable, friendly colour, and one you feel at home with, although brown still reminds us of the cat's wild origins. These cats really seem to want to communicate with you, through play, affectionate demonstrations, or 'conversation'. They appear to be wise cats, self-assured with a great sense of fun, and more often than not affectionate. A respected and loved brown cat is an excellent companion. This is a sincere and frank colour, the colour of the earth; it makes you feel comfortable with yourself.

THE CAT: Lilac

Represents sophistication and the unusual

Another colour associated with pedigree cats, this colour really is different and quite special. It is a sort of pinky grey, a sophisticated and pretty colour, suggesting sweetness, fantasy and an ethereal essence. Lilac cats appear to have a childlike quality; they remind us of 'sugar and spice and all things nice', and even if we do not associate them with their wild cousins, they are nevertheless very much *cats*. They appear to be aware of their unique colour, leading them to be a little 'bossy' at times. They are full of fun and mystery, bright, friendly cats which are usually very affectionate and have a definite character of their own – but are not always as innocent as they appear. They have a beauty with a unique, dreamlike quality about it.

THE CAT: Ticked and Spotted Patterns

Represents the wild

These cat patterns are evocative of the wild cats. The Egyptian Mau, Spotted Oriental Shorthair, and the Ocicat are spotted cats and are a variation of the tabby pattern.

The Abyssinians and Somalis have a ticked coat pattern which is called agouti, each hair banded with two or more

Eqyptian Mau with Foreign white

dark bands. Agouti is the underlying pattern of tabbys, on which the solid colour pattern is superimposed. The agouti coat pattern is more commonly found in wild cats than domestic ones. Because spotted and ticked cats are so close to their wild cousins in appearance it is perhaps the nearest we can come to living with the image of a wild cat. Although affectionate and enjoying human company, some of these cats also have a great need to fulfil their feline instincts; their love of freedom often causes them to range over wide areas, spending a great deal of time hunting. Possessing beauty and power, they are also often very affectionate to one special member of their human family, sharing with them their secrets and love of life.

Once you have studied your favourite coat colours and patterns, you can go on to examine what each of these implies about your own personality.

THE CAT OWNER: *Ginger and Cream, including Red Tabby*

A colour often chosen by boys. They may be trying to identify with their own male consciousness. In choosing a ginger-coloured cat it is probable that people empathise with the cat's image of energy. This colour of cat might attract a spirited person, direct and enthusiastic, with drive and lots of energy. On the other hand, it may be that a rather placid person, who longs to be able to express her emotions, will choose a ginger cat to represent the part of herself she feels is inhibited, delighting in her cat's display of agility and spirit. Remember that energy does not have to be expressed physically; it can be mental energy, or expressed through creativity. People choosing this colour may have a quick temper and be inclined to impatience, but equally quick to offer love and comfort.

Hopefully their sense of humour will always prevail, making them good companions for their ginger cats.

THE CAT OWNER: Tortoiseshell Pattern and Tri-coloureds (Black, Red and White)

People attracted to tortoiseshell and tri-coloured cats may feel more comfortable with the gentle side of life; this is not surprising as these cats represent the feminine principle. Hopefully they use their kind and sensitive nature to its full advantage. They may tend to be over-emotional, but their imaginative side can be used in a creative way. Do not forget that tortoiseshell and tri-coloured cats are full of mischief, and as this also reflects the owner, I shall leave it to the reader to interpret how it is manifested.

As tortoiseshell and tri-coloureds are often considered good luck, it seems natural to assume that these cats have a comfortable feel about them, and that people favouring this colour prefer a quiet life. Even if they haven't yet managed to attain this, their cat's comforting image is a symbol of what they desire.

THE CAT OWNER: *Grey and Brown Tabby Pattern*

This is one of the hardest patterns to interpret, because
people attracted to this pattern may be so different in
character and outlook. As tabby is the base of all domestic
cat coat patterns, anyone attracted to these cats may be as
diverse in nature as any of the cat's qualities. The tabby,
however, has a very strong wild cat resemblance, and
perhaps people who choose this cat have a similarity in
that they are all strongly pulled to the wild image with
its sense of freedom and power.

The owners of these cats may well be artistic – after all,
the tabby pattern is very beautiful. The self-contained feel
of a tabby may also be appreciated by the tabby owner
who may have an affinity with this.

Stability and independence are things I feel are important to the tabby owner, as well as a connection with the
wild from the comfort of the home; a tabby has a feel of
always being there, and possibly its owner is in need of
security and enjoys company.

THE CAT OWNER: *Grey and Blue*

The owner of a grey cat may have a desire to be different:
elegant and sophisticated, with an almost regal air. Such
people may be careful in choosing friends, making the
most of their talents and often putting in a lot of work
along one line of activity. This could be the result of a

grey cat person being a little detached and consequently concentrating on an activity that absorbs his or her energies. Grey seems to reflect two main characteristics: one is calmness and a laid-back attitude – a cool cat; the other, depression – I'm feeling blue. Either of these feelings could reflect a grey cat owner. Some people may choose a grey cat to calm their otherwise busy and hectic lives, enabling them to be in touch with their own inner calm. Sometimes, if a grey cat owner has a rather bland, indifferent air, he or she will be hiding a slight nervousness and may need time to accept change and make new friends.

THE CAT OWNER: Black

The closest of all the colours to the unconscious, black represents darkness, those things we do not yet know. It also represents the female element. In choosing a black cat people may be fascinated by the spiritual and mystical part of their own nature, and have a desire to understand their unconscious and its mysteries, or simply to live alongside it without feeling that it is a threat. Without a doubt, a fit black cat is very beautiful. The silhouette of the cat shows so clearly that its shape can be admired to the fullest. So we may assume that those who choose to own a black cat may well have an appreciation of beauty.

Black cats are reported to be full of mischief, and perhaps their owners can understand this. Of all the cats the black ones appear to be the most self-contained, a quality that may also be part of their owner's own personality.

THE CAT OWNER: *Black and White*

Black and white together are a symbol of balance and harmony, so maybe people choosing this cat feel that order is important to them. I would not be surprised to learn that they were good listeners, for the black and white cats with whom they identify have a solid, dependable feel about them. I have told more of my troubles to a black and white cat than to any other colour, feeling it somehow understood and would not be disturbed by it. There are other aspects of a black and white cat with which the owner may have an affinity: one is the cat's reputation for a sense of humour, and another is its smart man-about-town appearance. They are reported to have either good or naughty temperaments, but how people perceive black and white cats' characters in general will probably depend on how they perceive themselves.

THE CAT OWNER: *White*

White represents illumination – to lighten our darkness. Black symbolises the unconscious, white awareness, yet despite this some people still feel afraid of white cats. It could be because we dress our ghosts in white, but we dress our gods and angels in it as well. Perhaps the white cat reminds us of aspects of ourselves we feel to be too far removed, things we don't understand, or are afraid of. People choosing a white cat may have a fear of the 'dark' side of themselves, so that they feel more comfortable with a white cat, or use a white cat to balance their own dark side as the villain in the James Bond novels appears to do.

A well-groomed white cat may have an owner who has a very meticulous nature, liking things kept clean, neat and tidy. This particularly applies to long-haired white cats. The white cat's clear-cut image is reminiscent of white porcelain, a delicate form of beauty, and perhaps white cat people can understand and appreciate fine art and this kind of delicacy. Because a beautiful white cat is such an elegant image, its owner may also enjoy being admired and may project onto this beautiful animal which accepts admiration with such poise and confidence.

THE CAT OWNER: Brown and Chocolate

Brown is the colour of 'Mother Earth' and causes a warm, comfortable, nurturing feeling. People choosing a brown cat may have a desire to be in touch with these aspects of their own personality, or may feel it reflects their own character. Because a plain brown cat is distinctive, its owner may have a strong sense of individuality. Such people probably enjoy the wildness of Cat, feeling this to be an essential part of the feline character. This preference is not so pronounced as in the owner of a ticked or spotted cat, but it is still an important factor, enabling the owner to feel in touch with the animal kingdom. Brown is a friendly colour and so it is possible brown cat people enjoy communicating and have a good sense of humour, as well as enjoying quiet, reflective moments.

THE CAT OWNER: *Lilac*

Lilac is a feminine colour, and these cats suggest sweetness, innocence and a delicate beauty. There are three main aspects of lilac that may draw people to choose one. The first is the feminine, pretty aspect; this may attract people strongly pulled to their own feminine qualities, or girls who are going through the stage of trying to establish their own self-awareness. People attracted to the gentle side of their nature may also find lilac cats attractive.

The next one is the sophisticated and unusual aspect of lilac cats; this will attract people who feel a need to be different, and who wish to express and display this desire and make it known. The third aspect is the lilac cat's dream-like, fantastical and ethereal quality. We all feel a need to be in touch with this aspect of ourselves from time to time, but if this is an important part of our personalities it may influence our selection of a lilac cat.

Anyone who has kept a lilac cat will assure you that despite their innocent appearance, they are just as full of mischief as cats of any other colour, if not more so, and the reasons for choosing another lilac may well change from those which existed when choosing the first one.

THE CAT OWNER: Ticked and Spotted Patterns

Any person choosing one of these cats as his or her companion must surely have a love of wild cats. Independence, strength and power are characteristics symbolised by wild cats. 'King of the Jungle' seems to sum this up. Perhaps ticked or spotted cat owners are very aware of these qualities within themselves, and have a respect for them.

It is possible that people choosing these cats may feel a little restricted by life, and through their cats they can enjoy a sense of freedom. An empathy with nature, the opportunity to feel at one with animals, is of great benefit both to ourselves and to the animals, and I feel people attracted to these cats may come very close to this.

As ticked and spotted cats are said to resemble the early Egyptian cats, it is possible that their owners have an affinity with the poise, self-confidence, mystery and power which the Ancient Egyptians saw and revered in their cats.

3

Choosing Your Cat by Type and Breed

What type of cat do you prefer – long-haired, short-haired, or a medium-haired breed like the Balinese? With pedigree cats there does seem to be a difference in the personality of each breed. This is because selective breeding ensures that personality traits are passed on genetically, from cat to kitten. A Persian and a Himalayan, for example, are both classed as Longhairs but differ noticeably in character, although they will have closer links than, say, a Persian and a Foreign. I have therefore grouped the breeds together under long-haired, medium-haired and short-haired cats, with a special group for the more unusual breeds.

Within each group I have examined some of the best known breeds, and you will see how the overall personality traits differ from group to group by the character summaries I have included at the end of each group. Take, for instance, a black Longhair and a black Foreign: although they will both possess all the attributes that distinguish black cats from those of other colours, the fact that the Longhairs are more placid than the Foreigns will subdue the black element, while the high energy of the Foreigns will highlight it.

I have based my descriptions of the cat characters on pedigree cats, but the same general principles apply to non-pedigree cats, although here the differences may not be quite so pronounced.

THE CAT: Long-haired Breeds

These include Persians, Chinchillas and Colourpoint Longhairs (Himalayans). Cats of these breeds have cobby bodies with thick, short legs, broad, round heads, small ears, full cheeks and very short noses. The stunning coat is long and silky in an array of beautiful colours, with a

Persian cat

ruff of longer hair. Long hair of this type is not found in wild cats.

Persians

The Persian's rather flat face often has a grumpy, no-nonsense expression, but in fact these cats are placid and gentle. They are easily able to adapt to new environments and are undemonstrative, with quiet voices.

Colourpoint Longhairs (Himalayans)

A Persian type of cat with Siamese colouring and marking. Their temperaments are described as being more enterprising than the normal Persian, but more placid than the vivacious and often demanding Foreign.

SUMMARY OF PERSONALITY

Long-haired breeds share placid, gentle temperaments. They are quiet, distinguished and not quite so demonstrative or demanding as Foreigns. They love to lie around looking beautiful and need constant brushing to keep them immaculate. They appear to be anything-for-a-quiet-life cats.

THE CAT: Medium-haired Breeds

A group including Birmans, Balinese, Angoras, Turkish and the Maine Coon. These breeds fall between the long-haired and short-haired cats and seem to have modified characters to match. They have sturdy body shapes but are longer and more lithe and elegant than a Persian, with longer legs and tail. They also have a longer head and larger ears.

Their coats are silkier and less fluffy than a Persian's and they do not require quite as much grooming – apart from the Angora and Turkish which moult heavily in summer, but are still easier to groom than Persians.

Birmans

Intelligent and affectionate, the Birman is not so placid as a Persian, and although it can be an active cat, it is not quite so full of mischief as a Siamese. Apart from white gloves on their paws, Birmans share the same markings as Siamese.

Balinese

The Balinese is like the Siamese in all respects apart from its long, close, silky coat. As these cats developed from the early Siamese they have similar characters. They are athletic, playful, demanding, intelligent and very affectionate.

Angoras

Bright, active cats. As kittens they develop early. They are intelligent and gentle. They moult very heavily in summer, and as they lick their fur, care should be taken that they do not get fur balls in their stomachs.

Turkish Cats

Known as the Turkish Van. They are very similar to Angora cats except that they have a different coat pattern – Turkish Vans have auburn patches on the head and an auburn tail. Their personalities are very similar to Angoras', although sometimes they are a little more highly strung. Breeders are working to rectify this, and both Angoras and Turkish Vans make very beautiful and graceful companions.

Maine Coon

Very large cats, believed by some to be a cross between Angoras and domestic cats. Some reports say they are

Turkish Van

shy and others that they have a perfect personality, bright and full of fun, entertaining their owners with charming clownish tricks.

SUMMARY OF PERSONALITY

All these cats share bright, intelligent personalities. They are gentle and affectionate, and some are a little shy. Not so placid as the Persians and not so extrovert as the Foreigns (apart from the Balinese), they are very equable characters.

THE CAT: British and American Short-haired Breeds

These are strong, sturdy cats with cobby bodies, full chests and short legs. They have large, round heads, well developed cheeks, short noses and small round ears with a good width between. A short, dense coat without harshness or woolliness is characteristic of this breed. If short-haired cats and long-haired cats could be grouped by temperament, the British and American Shorthairs would be in the same group as Persians, and the Balinese, Angoras and other oriental Longhairs would be classed with the Foreigns. In other words, the shape and temperament of British and American Shorthairs is closer to Persians than to Foreigns.

British and American Shorthairs include British Blue, Silver Tabby, Chartreux and British Tipped Shorthair, and possess a wide range of rich and beautiful colours

– Pedigree Red Tabby and all the Tabby colours, Black Smoke, Blue-Cream, Black, Bi-Coloured, Tortoiseshell and Blue. They would normally include Manx and Scottish Folds, but I have grouped these in a separate section entitled Unusual Breeds. The pedigree Shorthair is a magnificent cat, with a strong body, thick fur and wonderful colouring.

British Blue

This cat is a perfect example of a British Shorthair, a beautiful bluish grey with a fine plush coat and a typical British Shorthair shape. Very intelligent and gentle.

Silver tabby

Silver Tabbies

These cats are show-stoppers, very beautiful. Classed as an American Shorthair, they are not so cobby as the British and have longer legs and larger ears. Strong in body and stamina with affectionate personalities, they make ideal, gentle pets.

SUMMARY OF PERSONALITY

All the Shorthairs seem to be quiet, hardy cats, affectionate, untemperamental, intelligent but not quite so mischievous as the Foreigns. They are also easy to groom and are good family companions.

THE CAT: *Foreign Short-haired Breeds*

'Foreign' does not mean the country of origin but rather the type of cat. Foreigns are elegant, slim cats with firm, muscular bodies, slender legs and long tails. Their head shape is more wedge than round and they have longer noses and larger eyes than British and American Shorthairs.

 Foreigns include Siamese, Burmese, Russian Blues, Korat, Abyssinians, Asians, Havanas, Orientals, Rex, Egyptian Mau, Ocicats, and Tonkinese. I shall look at just a few of these.

Siamese

Very beautiful, elegant cats with extrovert personalities. Very intelligent, they quickly learn to retrieve and walk on leads. They are very close to their human companions, demanding and giving lots of affection and company, and pining if this is suddenly withdrawn. Active and athletic, they can be noisy and respond to their owners with loud cat-chat. Life with a Siamese is not dull. They make bright, devoted, wonderful companions.

Burmese

Very similar to a Siamese in temperament but more 'laid back'; very athletic, adaptable, intelligent and playful. They will also retrieve if taught to do so and are quick to learn new games. If given the chance they love to ride around on their human companion's shoulders – and swing on the curtains! They are very affectionate and often favour their owners with little kisses. A Burmese is a joy to be with, besides being extremely beautiful.

Asians

A Burmese and Chinchilla cross, but more Burmese than Chinchilla. They have a Burmese personality and shape but with a wonderful tipped coat and green eyes.

Abyssinian

These are one-people cats which do not take easily to living in large cat groups. They are affectionate and gentle, and very beautiful with their stunning ticked coat. They attract a lot of attention at cat shows and I do not know of a single 'cat person' who does not agree on the beauty of the Abyssinian. Of all domestic cats, it most closely resembles a wild cat. Although they can be a little highly strung and may be inclined to roam, Abyssinians are very intelligent and make wonderful companions for their special person.

SUMMARY OF PERSONALITY

All the Foreigns seem to have similar characters. They are cats with a capital C: extremely affectionate, demonstrative and active, showing ingenuity and great intelligence. They are very attached to their human companions, whose company they will demand and who will receive their devotion in return.

Manx cat

THE CAT: *Unusual Breeds*

These unusual cats would normally be grouped with Shorthairs or Foreigns, but because they are so different from normal cats, I felt that they deserved special consideration in a group of their own.

Unusual breeds include Cornish and Devon Rex, Manx, Japanese Bobtail, Scottish Fold and Sphynx.

Cornish and Devon Rex

These are the curly-coated cats that people seem either to love or to dislike. Although the Rex is the result of a mutation in a British-type domestic cat, its shape is distinctly Foreign. The Cornish and Devon Rex are now recognised as separate breeds. They are affectionate, intelligent, agile and fun-loving. Their whiskers are curly and their wavy coats have a lovely plush feel to them. As they do not moult as much as normal-coated cats they do not need much grooming, but because their coats are not as thick as other Shorthairs they need protection from extreme weather conditions.

Manx

The distinctive feature of this cat is its lack of tail, although in fact tailless cats appear throughout the world, probably as a result of mutations. The Manx also has a special double coat made up of a glossy top coat and a thick, soft undercoat. Its overall body shape should be well rounded (not fat) with a rounded head. If you want to breed Manx you must first read up very carefully about their genes, for if these are not studied you may find that the cats are being wrongly matched, resulting in a high proportion of still-births and malformations. For all the problems, the Manx has a devoted following and makes an intelligent, affectionate and unusual companion.

The Scottish Fold

A cat whose ears are folded forward and downward, resulting in a sad expression. Cats with drooping ears have been reported for centuries, but the breed known as the Scottish Fold originated in Scotland in 1961. They are strong, hardy cats and have a reputation for being placid and well balanced. Happy, loving cats, they have characteristics similar to those of the British and American Shorthairs.

SUMMARY OF PERSONALITY

The cats in this group differ a little in their characters, but what they do all have in common is their unusual appearance, and this is what has the greatest influence on our impressions of them.

As you have seen, each type and breed of cat has its own personality traits. So how are these qualities reflected in the character of you, the owner?

THE CAT OWNER: Long-haired Breeds

The owners of long-haired cats may be attracted to them because they see in these cats a physical resemblance to themselves – well-rounded features or long and elaborate hair styles. I love to walk round the Longhair section of a cat show and look at some of the hair styles of Longhair owners. At a recent show I visited I was delighted to see an owner who had long, very bushy blonde hair, and her cat was a Longhair Cream. A well-groomed Longhair lies about and appears to enjoy the fuss and admiration it receives on its appearance. Perhaps this is something that appeals to a Longhair owner and reflects the way she sees herself.

Long-haired cats usually have placid, gentle temperaments and undemanding natures, which could also reflect the character of the owner who may feel a little nervous about being challenged and may prefer a quiet life, needing to feel in control of the situation; Longhairs, after all, give the impression that they are equal to any eventuality. Often this kind of cat is mothered and fussed over, and the fact that they need grooming every day suggests that the owner needs to satisfy a nurturing instinct. A healthy, well-groomed Longhair is certainly a credit to its owner's caring and meticulous nature.

THE CAT OWNER: Medium-haired Breeds

It is possible that people who are attracted to this kind of cat are pulled by the visual image of a Longhair, while at the same time being attracted by the more extrovert personality of the Foreign breeds. It may be that their personalities are more inclined towards the Foreigns, while their lives are so busy that the visual image of a peaceful, easy-going cat seems more appealing. Or it could be that the bright, affectionate and sometimes shy characters of these cats suit people who have middle-of-the-road temperaments and simply wish to avoid extremes.

The cat's beauty also cannot fail to be an attraction to the medium-haired cat owner; it is neither the ostentatious appeal of a Persian nor the lithe, sensual loveliness of a Foreign, but a more gentle, delicate and subtle beauty that the owner may recognise and feel drawn to.

THE CAT OWNER: British and American Short-haired Breeds

These strong, sturdy cats are bound to attract people who enjoy self-contained, no-nonsense, healthy cats. Perhaps they are the most independent of all the cat owners and are able to respect this aspect of their cats.

The short-haired breeds seem to be quiet, untemperamental and intelligent, so make ideal companions for people who share those attributes.

Shorthairs are the epitome of the family cat: curled up by the hearth or waiting by a mouse hole, they have an eternal, comfortable and homely feel. This reassuring image of Cat offers its human companions security and a sense of well-being and companionship. It has a stabilising and relaxing effect on the owners, and maybe they recognise that their cats are fulfilling a basic need in themselves. These owners may be interested in the spiritual or mystical side of their lives and be lovers of natural beauty. Shorthairs are very much the basic Cat archetype; they symbolise all the Cat attributes.

If it is the cat's independent image that attracts their owners, they may be keen to share life with a cat companion while respecting its Cat nature.

THE CAT OWNER: Foreign Short-haired Breeds

While Shorthair owners in general may respect Cat nature, people who are attracted to Foreigns delight in it, enjoying the mischievous fun of the cat. These owners probably have a keen sense of humour or are inclined to be rebellious – or both. After all, this type of cat doesn't necessarily do what it's told or meant to do but rather what it *wants* to do. It is a great inspiration for those who feel inhibited in any way or who revel in this individualistic attitude.

These cats have two distinct qualities: one is a slinky, mysterious aura that is evocative of Eastern spirituality and the unknown; the other is an extremely affectionate, intelligent nature, characteristic of an active, high-energy cat, showing a great deal of ingenuity. People attracted to Foreigns may be recognising one or both of these aspects in themselves.

Foreigns also give themselves devotedly to their human companions, which may fill a gap of loneliness. There is no doubt that Foreigns are very beautiful with their sleek, sensual and elegant lines, and their co-ordinated, panther-like movements. Anyone who chooses one of these cats must surely have an affinity with and appreciation of the beauty of nature.

THE CAT OWNER: Unusual Breeds

These cats are highly individual in appearance, and a sense of individuality combined with a desire to be different is probably a strong reason for choosing one of them; the owner will probably also have a keenly discerning affinity with the unusual. The fact that these cats are so strikingly different in appearance compared to ordinary cats could mean they evoke a desire to nurture and protect. Scottish Folds, for instance, have a sad expression, and Devon Rex have an appealing wide-eyed, innocent look. These special breeds may therefore attract owners who project their own vulnerability onto their cats, and by caring for the cats they are able to respond to some of their own emotional needs.

There is another side, however, and that is the pioneering spirit that is needed to develop and breed these unusual cats. As long as the cat's health and welfare is of *paramount importance*, it may satisfy a person who needs a challenging experience, to breed a fit and happy unusual cat. But if what is produced is cats which have defects that cause them pain and suffering, then it is better if this pioneering spirit and desire to be different is satisfied by other means.

4

Your Cat and You – The Psychology of Your Relationship

Why we choose a particular cat as a companion and how we relate to it says a lot about ourselves. Let's look at some of the underlying psychology which can illuminate our own personalities and explain the essential nature of our relationship with our cats.

Projection

When you feel love or care for a person or an animal, you are recognising something of yourself in them at the physical or emotional level, or at both levels. Projection then takes place, which means that you project your feelings onto them. Without projection there would be no love or caring, because we can only relate to others through our own experiences; our only concepts of love, pain, hunger, cold, warmth, joy and sadness come from what we ourselves know. It would be impossible to imagine pain if you had not felt it, or to visualise colours if you had always been blind, or to understand music if you had never been able to hear. When we care for others, we therefore see them through the filter of our own experience and project onto them our own feelings. We are not aware of this process; it is an unconscious act, but also an act of unity, a recognition of the non-separateness of the individual. If you isolated yourself from projection in order to avoid the complications that might arise, then the desire to care for those around you would cease.

The ideal way to use projection is to respect and honour everyone else's individuality, while at the same time being aware that underneath that individuality we are all part of a system of interdependent being. Then we respect and care for each other and all living things, and in doing so we also respect and care for ourselves. One could say that projection is an individualised expression of the general concept that we are all one. All our relationships with others are based on projection, with either positive or negative results. It follows that what you are projecting, and onto whom, tells you a lot about yourself.

For a projection to be positive and beneficial, you must remain aware that another being is involved. If you should lose sight of that, projection can become a negative process, since you then try to take over the person or animal emotionally and project onto it your own fears and anxieties as well as your caring. Its personality becomes entwined with yours, so that its actions, positive or negative, affect the way you perceive and feel about yourself. You see it as part of you, and the fact that this part seems largely out of your control leads to feelings of helplessness and frustration. We all tend to assume that those we are close to will behave in the same fashion as ourselves and are often surprised when they do not.

The classic example of this process is the way we treat our children. We may try to impose our wishes on our child by making him take subjects at school which neither interest him nor suit him; *we* like the subject, so he must, too. When he tells us than there is a different subject he would rather study, if it is one we cannot relate to, we automatically try to steer him towards our own preference – to his detriment. And if we extend this blindness to embrace our feelings about hairstyles, clothes, music and friends, then the problems can multiply almost infinitely. There has to be some parental control, guided by the logic and common sense which the child may not yet have developed, but the line between this and the imposition of our own personal preferences can be a very thin one.

This principle can also apply to your relationship with your cat and is particularly apparent in those who breed for show purposes. Much thought and effort go into producing a good show cat; on the positive side this includes the cat's physical and emotional condition, and well-planned breeding takes into account the welfare of the cat. However, this is not always the case, and in the process of trying to achieve significantly larger, longer, fatter, thinner or prettier cats, some breeders – clearly obsessed with personal achievement – are in danger of totally losing sight of the real essence of Cat. So at the end of this selective breeding process they may well wind up with cats that are interbred, highly strung and susceptible to illness. And that is bad news for Cat! As with humans, you must project onto your cat in a positive way, so that you can love and care for it as a respected companion, without either of you losing your own identity.

I encountered a perfect example of positive projection when I was finding homes for a litter of Hooli's kittens. I had two kittens left, and since I intended to keep one of them anyway, I was not very worried; I knew that a good home for the last kitten would turn up eventually. No sooner had I reached this conclusion than the telephone rang. The caller was a woman named Norma who had seen my advertisement. Had we any kittens left, she enquired, and if so, could she and her husband Fred come over to see them straight away? She had a nice voice, and after a few minutes' conversation about cats I felt that she was likely to make a good owner.

An hour later the couple arrived at my door. I was pleased with them: both seemed to have a very gentle, caring manner, along with a keen sense of humour and a definite, cat-orientated personality. They had kept cats for many years, but having had one or two litters from their last Siamese cat, they were now catless and were missing feline company. Fred had brought his camera and, delighted with the kittens, was soon busy taking photographs. My other cat, William, not to be outdone by the kittens in popularity, managed to get himself into every shot. Norma asked if they could have both kittens, explaining that they never kept a cat on its own as they felt it was better for the cat to have a companion to play with.

Of course Norma was right, and I was happy that Be-Be and Bessle, as they were to be called, would stay together and enjoy each other's company, despite my regrets that I would not be able to keep one of them for myself. At least I had the consolation that Be-Be and Bessle would stay with me for another month, since Norma and Fred had just moved into a cottage that was being renovated, and they wanted to get it organised before the kittens were introduced.

As it turned out, we were all to become close friends. We found that we had a lot of interests in common, and I was able to see Be-Be and Bessle regularly, and watch them grow into beautiful and happy cats. Norma and Fred treated them with love and respect. As they were both at home for most of the time, the kittens were given lots of attention, with Fred continually thinking up new games for them. The couple's loving, lively and intelligent personalities seemed to project onto the kittens which, feeling secure, have grown into confident and intelligent cats.

Both Norma and Fred recognise that cats are cats in their own right, and while neither is completely free from anxieties (who is?) they do not project these onto their cats. If the cats ever sense and seem affected by their anxieties – as most cats close to their owners are capable of doing – they reassure them by giving them extra attention and cuddles. This has the effect of helping both cats and humans to relax.

The balance that Norma and Fred have achieved is very positive, but it has not happened by accident. Both have taken an interest in self-understanding, Norma using hers in a practical way through drama therapy. But one thing is certain: what they have learnt, and are still learning, they are using in their lives, and the cats are benefiting from the process.

In many ways animals share our capacity for feeling – for it is clear that they feel pain, joy, happiness and sorrow – and the average person projects onto them quite naturally. Pets play a valuable part in our lives – indeed, those of you who have found life a difficult experience, especially in your childhood, and whose ego (or sense of individuality and self-esteem) has not had a chance to develop fully, may feel insecure in the company of people and more at peace with the unthreatening world of animals. You may find it much easier to project onto animals, and both you and your pet will find comfort in caring for each other.

Sometimes, however, under certain circumstances, you may be unable to project onto animals. This can happen if you have had negative experiences and, without realising it, have shut yourself off from your own feelings in order to protect yourself from a world you unconsciously view as hostile. Your need to arm yourself against further hurt may lead you to detach yourself from both people and animals; but if you can make the effort to form a link with an animal, you may find that your trust in life gradually opens up again.

On the other hand, some of you who have had negative

experiences may become strongly motivated to remove the pain of others; because you yourself have suffered, you are able to use this in projection instead of suppressing it. This motivation can often be found amongst those working actively for child welfare organisations and animal charities.

Animals as a whole greatly benefit from positive projection which helps their experience and awareness to grow, and if you have ever kept a companion animal with which you have been close, you will realise that it is not a one-way process! The animal is also projecting onto you, completing the circle of love so that you both benefit and, in turn, so do those around you.

Bereavement

Whatever your relationship with your cat may be, because its life-span is not as long as yours, sooner or later you will have to face its death. For various reasons this can be a very traumatic experience.

Sometimes your cat may be the only companion you have; it becomes the focus of your life, an extension of yourself, and gives you a reason to live. You have to feed and look after it, and it responds by showing you love and making you feel wanted and needed. This relationship is of great benefit both physically and psychologically. At the death of your cat companion you may feel that your life is literally falling apart. You may experience the kind of loss, and need as much care and help, as if you had lost a human companion.

If the identity of the object of projection – your cat – becomes unconsciously entangled with yours, when it falls ill or dies your perspective is distorted and you feel as if a piece of yourself has been lost.

You can help yourself to ease some of your very natural pain and confusion by trying to see your cat as a separate being, apart from yourself. I don't mean that you should not grieve for it; of course you will miss the companionship and happiness your cat friend has brought you, and will feel all the normal symptoms associated with grief. But if you already understand some of the processes that go on in your relationship with your cat, and can see it as an individual to be loved and respected as such, some aspects of the pain, at least, will be easier to bear.

The grief you feel may be complicated by other emotions. If the cat was formerly the beloved pet of someone who has died and with whom you were very close, you may unconsciously have identified the cat with the person you have lost. While the cat lived you still had a part of that person with you – in a sense he or she was still alive; now, perhaps for the first time, you have to face the fact that your loved one is no longer with you and so your grief is intensified.

It would help if families and friends were aware that this can happen, so that they could give bereaved people more attention and support than they might normally do on the death of a pet.

Children may project onto a cat the role of brother or sister, confiding in it, sharing with it their secrets, things they cannot or would not tell their parents. They may use the cat as a playmate and the cat in turn will provide comfort, company and love, which may not always be

forthcoming from their parents. At its death they will need special understanding.

If as a couple you have shared the love and happiness of a cat companion and your partner has died first, then when the cat dies you will feel renewed grief for the loss of your partner. The cat was a link between you – after all, you had both shared the joy of caring for it and you know that now he or she would also have shared your grief. Your need for your partner is reawakened and you find yourself grieving both for the cat and for your loved one.

Often the death of a loved cat is not understood by other people as a pain serious enough to warrant special care and consolation. This is a mistake, for whatever role your cat filled, it was loved and its death has left a gap.

While a cat is with you, you have a living symbol of aspects of yourself. Through your cat you can experience vicariously things you may not be able to do, or places where you may be unable to go. Think of your cat up a tree, or of its ability to find warm, sunny spots and, without cares or worries, just to settle and doze. You can share its independence and self-containedness. It is a vision of beauty, with a grace that has an arrogance of its own. It seems to sense just the right place to pose and be adored, like a living work of art that is able to inform the landscape.

Your cat enables you to make contact with animals and learn from them, to respect them as individuals and communicate with them by love and caring. All these things play their part in giving you a more balanced psyche.

With all these benefits and the fun and joy that living

with your cat can bring, it is obvious that at its death you will experience a very real grief.

The Unconscious

The unconscious is the part of the mind which is not normally accessible to consciousness, although it still affects behaviour. As well as the personal unconscious there is a collective unconscious which acts as a psychological framework within which we all operate.

In choosing a cat you are being pulled by your unconscious, and studying what kind of cat you choose – as regards breed, colour, personality and gender – can tell you a lot about the hidden aspects of yourself. After the cat has been in close contact with you for a while, some of its behaviour patterns can also give you a greater understanding of yourself.

Within the unconscious it is possible to perceive animals as symbols of either male or female elements. We can explore these possibilities through the use of keywords.

Cat keywords

Female, passive, mystical, spiritual, reflective, creative, introvert, night, moon, intuition, sensitivity, emotion, UNCONSCIOUS.

Dog keywords

Male, active, logical, earthy, energetic, aggressive, extrovert, day, sun, reason, sense, mind, CONSCIOUS.

It follows from this that people who choose cats as companions probably feel close to, and comfortable with, the unconscious side of their nature. Although Cat represents the collective unconscious, it also has a female aspect and because of this women find it easier to relate to, as they have a conscious image of Cat and of themselves as female. Men, on the other hand, are facing their unconscious on both levels, so fewer men own cats. However, those who do own a cat are more likely to have a well-balanced acceptance of both the male and female aspects in their nature.

COLLECTIVE UNCONSCIOUS: FEMALE SYMBOL

Cat represents the collective unconscious, the cat is evocative of the mystical, spiritual, intuitive and emotional side of our nature, which lies in our unconscious.

WOMAN'S PERSONAL IMAGE OF CAT

Woman can relate to Cat more easily than man because her conscious image is female.

MAN'S PERSONAL IMAGE OF CAT

To man Cat represents the collective unconscious and also his own unconscious feminine image, so he may find cat more difficult to relate to.

WOMAN'S CONSCIOUS IMAGE: FEMALE

A female cat to a woman represents the collective unconscious and is also a feminine symbol, so a woman finds this cat easier to relate to.

MAN'S CONSCIOUS IMAGE: MALE

While a male cat and some of his character represents a conscious male image to a man, his overall cat nature is still feminine and is also aligned to the collective unconscious.

WOMAN'S UNCONSCIOUS MALE IMAGE (HER ANIMUS)

While a male cat still represents the collective unconscious, his masculinity represents the unconscious male image in woman, but his overall cat nature is still a feminine symbol.

MAN'S UNCONSCIOUS FEMALE IMAGE (HIS ANIMA)

A female cat represents man's unconscious female image, and the collective unconscious.

Every human being contains both male and female elements. In the Glossary to Jung's book *Memories, Dreams, Reflections*, there is a very clear exposition of this concept:

> This psychological bisexuality is a reflection of the biological fact that it is the larger number of male (or female) genes which is the decisive factor in the determination of sex. The smaller number of contrasexual genes seems to produce a corresponding contrasexual character, which usually remains unconscious.

A woman's conscious image of herself will therefore be female. Her masculine nature will be unconscious (her animus).

A man's conscious image of himself will be male. His feminine nature will be unconscious (his anima).

To a greater or lesser degree the animus or anima filters through to the consciousness, and an understanding of its influence is very useful. If a woman chooses a female cat it is closer to her conscious image, while a male cat is closer to her unconscious male image. With a man, a male cat represents his conscious image, and a female cat represents his unconscious female image. A female cat will show you the female in yourself, and a male cat will show you the male element (see diagram opposite). If you choose both male and female cats, it is possible to study the balance of the male and female elements within yourself.

The process of choosing a cat reflects the changing

balance within the person making the choice. This balance involves elements of male and female, conscious and unconscious, and as the balance shifts during the person's life, so will the type of cat chosen also be different. The story of Elinor, in Chapter 1, illustrates this very clearly.

Cat clearly represents a very strong link with the unconscious, and in choosing one as your companion, you are affirming the importance of this element in your life. It may not be the dominant aspect in your experience, but you clearly feel attracted to it at a very deep level, and you can probably recognise in yourself one or more of the cat keywords.

Cats represent the unknown, the untamed. You never really *completely* know your cat. Although it enjoys your company, food and attention, to a certain degree it still walks alone, and is surrounded by an aura of mystery – just like your unconscious.

This sense of mystery associated with the unconscious has been expressed in the image of the cat in art through-out the ages. Art is born from the unconscious, and cats have been an inspiration to artists, poets and creative thinkers, including T. S. Eliot, Edward Lear, Manet, Renoir, Goya and Picasso.

Many stories have been written in which a cat (more than any other animal) is the talking companion on trips of time travel, mystery, magic, and fantasy. They are somehow compatible with our creative abilities. Great writers have used cats in their literature and have often anthropomorphised them. What makes this fiction seem plausible is that the cat symbolises aspects of ourselves and more often than not is placed in a role to which we unconsciously relate.

People who do not easily identify with animals often complain of the tendency of pet owners to anthropomorphise their pets. If an owner has projected human characteristics onto his or her pet, to the point of damaging the animal's own welfare, I can understand this point of view. But I often feel that people who are emphatically opposed to this habit are in danger of forgetting that we, too, are animals, and share a lot of traits, both physical and emotional, with our animal companions. By understanding the symbolic significance of cats in literature we are more able to understand ourselves.

In 1931 Lewis Carroll's book *Alice's Adventures in Wonderland* was censored by the authorities in China, because they considered it wrong that animals and humans should be portrayed as being on the same level, and that the animals should talk in human language.

Looking at events taking place in China at that time, a possible explanation for this attitude can be suggested. The country was in the middle of a triangular struggle, between the Nationalist party, led by Chiang Kai-shek (who desired a unified and independent China under a Nationalist government), the Japanese militarists who wished to control and dominate China, and the Communists led by Mao Tse-Tung. The people had to be held together, to work as a unit in a harsh, tough world where masculine energy was of prime importance. They had to face the hard outward reality of life, not the inward reflective side of human nature –

the compassionate, feminine side. *Alice* was fantasy, which might stimulate people to examine this gentler side and come face to face with the different parts of themselves. If they considered animals to be equal with humans, where would that lead? If to a softer and more feeling attitude, this would not be welcomed, when what was needed was discipline, and hard attitudes within an effective military structure. I am not saying that this was the only reason why those in power condemned the book, or that this was the conscious motive for banning it, but there is a possibility that it contributed to their decision. It makes an interesting speculation.

One of the significant points about *Alice's Adventures in Wonderland* and *Through the Looking Glass* is that Alice's pets are cats. One called Dinah is with her at the beginning of the first book, and by the beginning of the second Dinah has had two kittens, Kitty and Snowdrop. Alice talks to the kittens and pretends that they answer her. She enters her world of fantasy by means of a tunnel, or through the mist of the looking glass. Lewis Carroll therefore sent Alice into the world of the unconscious with two powerful symbols, so it is fitting that he should have given her cats as her real-life companions.

Another relatively recent and important tale is Rudyard Kipling's *The Cat that Walked by Himself*. Here we begin with all the animals in an untamed state, but the wildest of all is the cat. 'He walked by himself and all places were alike to him.' (What a symbol of the unconscious!) Man is also wild and only when he meets woman does he start to become tame. Working together they begin to make a more comfortable life. Within a warm, dry cave, with a fire that throws light over the surrounding area, they roast mutton and the woman makes a singing magic.

The first of the animals creeps up out of the forest – a dog, man's first friend – and wishes to sit by the fire and share the mutton bone. He asks the cat to join him but the latter declines the offer and prefers to walk alone, although he is always in the background watching what is going on. The dog goes to the woman, and in return for mutton bones he has to agree to help the man to hunt and to guard the cave by night. 'Ah,' says the cat who has been listening, 'although the woman is wise she is not as wise as I am!' But dog crawls into the cave, lays his head on the woman's lap, calls her his friend and agrees to her conditions.

One by one more wild things become tamed; each time they invite the cat to join them, but he just watches from a distance.

Eventually the cat sees that it would be advantageous to live with the woman, as she has warm cow's milk to drink and a comfortable cave to live in. He bargains with her: if he causes her to praise him three times, he will be allowed to share the cave but will not be tamed. He sets about winning her praise, and succeeds in living in the cave with his warm milk, by the warm fire. But the woman reminds him that the bargain was struck only with her, and that man and the dog will never fully accept him.

Here the cat is a beautiful symbol of the unconscious:

it can never be fully tamed, has a will of its own, but can work very well for the good of the whole when respected and listened to. There is nothing to fear in allowing this to happen, because you are still in control and have the ultimate say in what you do. If the unconscious is repressed or suppressed or ignored, it will often find a way of manifesting itself, of having a say, in a far from pleasant way.

The cat is able to come to terms with the woman (the unconscious also being a feminine symbol). They are able to respect and understand each other and the cat proves that the woman really does need him. The woman quite rightly says to the cat that the male side of mankind (her husband) can never succumb fully to the cat (the female), and neither can the dog (also a male symbol). So cat and woman are paired together, as are dog and man.

Another aspect of the tale is that woman tames the wild animals with her singing magic. This could be translated as her understanding, manipulating and directing the instincts with her feminine, passive, inward power. She harnesses them to help her husband who is the active, outward energy of the relationship. The cat she cannot tame, although she does come to an understanding with him and is closer to him than the man will ever become. Once the man and woman work in harmony they make life more comfortable for each other. This particular tale is a very interesting one to study.

Literature is full of symbols, and once you start to notice

them, fairy-tales and myths take on a new meaning and can become addictive. You may find yourselves browsing through your children's bookshelves and reading with renewed interest.

5

How You Treat Your Cat and What This Can Tell You

One of the most obvious ways of seeing projection at work is by examining how you look after your pet. This applies not only to cats but also to dogs. Take a look into a poodle parlour, with its range of haircuts and colours specially designed for the pet. But where in all this is the dog? He is lost under the owner's projection. If the dog is still given care, exercise and companionship he may be none the worse, and in some ways, by becoming a projection of his owner the animal can benefit, giving the owner the chance to express his or her feelings of love and caring.

The dog may also require a coat, and these coats now come in many styles: tartan, macho, camouflage, printed with cartoons, even decorated with frills and bows. The style is completely irrelevant to the dog but is an obvious projection of the owner, and it isn't difficult to see some of the characteristics of the owner being expressed in the choice.

Projection is reflected not only in the way you equip your pets but also in the way you treat them. There is considerable evidence that people who ill-treat animals are likely to be negative towards people as well. So the owner of a contented, happy cat is likely to be a kind and thoughtful person, not only in her relationship with her cat but also towards other people. Of course, if the cat is of a nervous nature due to genetic factors, traumatic events in its life or ill-health, even the kindest person may have a problem in trying to make it happy. Cats can and do respond to being cared for, however, and with patience sometimes even the most nervous cat can become confident and contented.

As the way you treat people, animals – even property – depends on your inner feelings, your cat can be a valuable mirror to give you an insight into your emotional life. This life is extremely diverse and complex, and I can only hope to cover the more obvious variations in the examples which follow.

1 Ignoring the Cat

If you are ignoring your cat when you would normally be very attentive to it, it is possible that you are well aware that you are going through an exceptionally busy and testing time, and that you are having to channel all your attention in one direction. On the other hand, you may not realise that your behaviour has changed; perhaps you have become too preoccupied to notice. Your cat, however, will certainly have noticed and may respond by showing less interest in you; you may find yourself ignored in turn. A cat needs its overtures of affection to be reciprocated, and if they are not, it will soon learn that there is nothing to be gained and will cease to bother with you. If your relationship was previously very close and it was very attached to you, it may suffer considerably, not understanding your sudden withdrawal of attention. It may even pine and refuse to eat, or begin to show neurotic symptoms. If matters have reached this stage, take it as a sign that you need to sit down without delay and consider all aspects of your own needs, not just those that are predominant, and also those of your cat. Remember that time spent with your cat can be very relaxing and rewarding – indeed it is most important for both of you. Not only does it help you to unwind, but it is the way to reinforce the bond between you.

I find it interesting to watch people's reactions when a cat enters the room. Some people act as if the cat does not exist, they simply ignore it. They obviously miss the joy and beauty that awareness of these lovely animals can bring. I'm not suggesting that they should have to enter into a commitment with the cat, merely that they could acknowledge it as a beautiful animal.

It could be that for them the cat signifies something which makes them block it out, or they may see it as a threat. The most obvious example of this is the cat's feminine image. For various reasons people may have distanced themselves from their own feminine aspect, possibly out of fear. I have known a number of people like this, all of them reacting as a result of early influences.

Henry springs particularly to mind. As a child he lived in a rather sterile home, ruled over by his mother who was a dragon of a woman, dominating both the boy and his father. In order for Henry to develop his own self-image he was faced with the hard task of detaching himself from his mother, who did not make it easy for him. In such circumstances many people would never detach themselves, and would remain under their mother's influence for life, their own masculine self-image never having a chance to develop fully. But Henry had a strong personality. At the first opportunity he left home and joined the armed forces where his conscious masculine image was encouraged. The power his mother unconsciously held over him, however, was never eradicated, just suppressed. So now, when Henry sees a cat which is not only feminine but also confident and arrogant, he may feel a little disturbed and the obvious way to avoid this is to ignore the cat.

Alison was brought up in a very different situation, although the end result was the same. Her father was the one who held the dominant position in her family, while her mother was a very gentle, quiet woman, lacking in inner strength. The person who had the most authority over Alison was her father, and he has also had the most influence on her life. Her masculine unconscious therefore became stronger than her feminine conscious self-image. After all, her father was successful, strong, full of energy and by far the more attractive parent on whom to model herself. The cat, with its feminine image, reminds her of her own feminine self, which could be confident and detached if she allowed it to develop, but her dominant masculine unconscious sees any such possibility as a threat to its authority. The familiar status quo, even if it is not fulfilling, makes her feel secure, whereas the threatening and difficult prospect of change fills her with unease. It is simpler to deny her conscious self by ignoring cats.

Ian represents yet another facet of early influence. Brought up in a secure family where he was the centre of attention, his interests and whims were indulged and he was encouraged to develop his individuality, always to be on top and to have a materialistic view of the world. His sensitivity was entirely neglected. The result was that his ego (self-esteem, self-awareness) became dominant, making it difficult for him to be in touch with his instincts, and he is now unable to project onto others, whether people or animals. He feels separate from them and as he has no empathy with cats, he ignores them.

These are not the only types of people to ignore cats but they do show how our environment, our experiences and perceptions of the world can influence the way we relate to people and animals.

2 Feeling Angry

If you are feeling angry with your cat for the most trivial reasons – reasons that would not normally be an issue – then it is time to look at yourself, because if you project onto your cat when you are feeling angry, you may take it out on him when it is really yourself you are angry with. For example, he might be miaowing for some food. This is something he normally does at his feeding time and you usually accept it and respond by feeding him. But today, because you are feeling touchy and choose to take it out on the cat, you may possibly ignore him, knowing that this will cause distress, or shout at him, or worse. Your cat will be upset, not knowing what he has done wrong. If you shout at him intermittently for doing things that would normally be accepted and rewarded, you may end up with a neurotic cat, causing problems for both the cat and yourself. Misdirected anger can be very destructive when inflicted on an innocent being – animal, child or adult – and for this reason it needs to be understood and dealt with in order to prevent suffering.

Anger is one of the ways in which dammed-up energy is released. It has become dammed up because you are inhibited by various conditions. Other people's needs and wishes, and society as a whole, contribute to your having to do things you may not like, or want to do. Your own fears and anxieties can inhibit you so greatly that you cannot allow yourself expression; consequently you become frustrated, and this often leads to anger.

In certain cases anger can be useful; it is a safety valve which blows when you haven't got the message and have gone on ignoring your own needs. It is also a means of self-defence, a way of protecting your interests.

Some people feel a great deal of anger – not the sort we all experience from time to time but the type that seems to be permanently bubbling under the surface, erupting at the slightest provocation. This type of anger usually stems from latent inhibitions controlled by fears, anxieties and frustrations, the foundations of which were laid down in childhood. These people often do not recognise this and may insist that the blame lies with conditions outside themselves. Certainly a person with this kind of anger can be helped by trying to understand what is going on in his or her unconscious.

Because anger is usually the result of not understanding, or not being able to fulfil, your own needs, it follows that once you understand the message behind the anger you are in a position to decide whether or not your needs can be satisfied. If they cannot, it is surprising how by just acknowledging them and reasoning with them the anger can subside.

3 Treating Your Cat with Respect

To treat your cat with love and respect and not subject it to your fears and anxieties is a very positive attitude. There are many people who love and care for cats, some giving up a great deal of their time in order to ease suffering and enhance the cats' lives.

A love of cats is just as informative of your inner self as a fear or dislike of them. An affinity with what they symbolise is a good start. Respecting their dignity and appreciating their companionship not only enriches your life but also your mind. If this respect is extended to cover all animals, including humans, then you have obtained a healthy balance, since the way you treat others is an indication of your inner self. Even if you find it difficult to relate to people and feel more comfortable in the company of animals, the fact that you treat animals with love and respect is a good basis for entering relationships with people as well. By not projecting your problems onto your cat, and by recognising it as an individual whose company you enjoy, with feelings and needs similar to yours, you and your cat will greatly benefit from each other's company.

4 A Desire to Nurture

A positive maternal projection is based upon the desire to nurture, meaning to care for, make happy and help to fulfil the life onto which you are projecting. Women in particular find this a strong drive, and in their case it probably is based on the maternal instinct; but if we use the word 'nurture' in its full sense, not just in its maternal context, then it becomes a function that applies equally to men. After all, to care for, make happy and help fulfil the life onto which you are projecting is the basic requirement of most relationships. In caring for others you are caring for yourself, and anyone treating a cat in this way is showing very natural feelings. This positive drive takes into account the cat's needs; the person benefits because the cat responds, and so both gain from this form of projection. Being sensible animals, cats lend themselves well to being nurtured and are very adept at nurturing in return.

5 Treating the Cat as a Child Substitute

This is quite different from just projecting a nurturing desire, because here you may lose sight of the fact that you are projecting onto a cat. And although some cats may lead a very comfortable and well-cared-for life as child substitutes, they will not receive full consideration of their own individual feline needs. How often we hear of cats being loved like human children, only to be neglected once a real child appears on the scene. I have known a cat pine to death because all the love and attention lavished on it was withdrawn when a baby was born. This is a very real danger for the cat, and if you truly profess to love and care for your cat you should not lose sight of its animal nature.

There is, however, a natural tendency to treat young animals as babies – which in fact they are; they may not be human ones, but the same commendable instinct which leads you to nurture and protect vulnerable infants moves you to nourish and care for baby animals, which are equally dependent on you. To feel needed and to form attachments is a basic healthy requirement of both humans and animals; we learn through relationships. But you have to remember that just as your children grow and you recognise them as individuals, so, too, do your companion animals. Even if they will always be dependent on you for their food, welfare, warmth and companionship, they will not always be your babies but will grow into your friends, with rights of their own. They are not material packages of your emotions which you can use or discard at will, but valuable friends with whom you can share your feelings and your homes, and who can help you satisfy some of your basic caring instincts.

6 Fear of Cats

Fear of cats can be based on a sound reason, such as having been badly bitten or attacked by a cat; or it may be inherited, passed on from parent to child. If your fear appears to have no logical base, however, it is possible that it may be caused by a deep-seated and irrational fear of the feminine, or other aspects of the self that cats may symbolise – for example, power, insight, magic, selfcontainedness, independence or the unconscious in general. A fear of the unconscious could be interpreted as resulting from feelings of insecurity, causing you to be irrationally afraid of things you do not know or which are beyond your control. Perhaps the pains, anxieties and fears locked away in your unconscious are very powerful, and because you feel you cannot understand them it gives these emotions a certain amount of control over you. Sometimes you may feel that if you hurt the cat you have projected onto, you will somehow alleviate the problem, but of course all that will happen is that an innocent cat will suffer, and the problem will remain unaltered.

Probably the best way of dealing with any fear is to try to understand it; it gives an opportunity to explore certain feelings and emotions. Another method of treating an animal phobia is called systematic desensitisation, a form of behaviour therapy. The patient is taught to relax and the feared stimulus – in this case the cat – is carefully and gradually introduced. At first the cat will be kept at a distance and only introduced for short periods, then slowly, as the patient becomes more able to relax in the cat's presence, the anxiety will subside; because anxiety and relaxation are incompatible, they cannot occur simultaneously. Although this is an effective way of easing your fears, it does not alter the fact that it is also useful and interesting to know and understand their basis.

7 Ill-treatment by Punishment

I believe that animals should not be punished in the conventional sense of the word. They do not understand why, and unless the punishment is administered while the animal is actually exhibiting undesirable behaviour it has no useful effect, in fact quite the contrary. Very often animals suffer greatly at the hands of people who use punishment to vent their own feelings rather than to change the animal's undesirable behaviour pattern. The result is usually an animal which has lost its spirit or developed neurotic symptoms.

Punishment is the most overused technique in animal training, and if its aim is to eliminate behaviour motivated by anxiety it is always counter-productive, since it will only increase the animal's anxiety. It can cause confusion because the animal will feel both attached to and afraid of its owner, and this conflict is bound to increase its neurosis still further. Despite the popular belief that cats do not need humans, they are in fact very attached to their owners. If we give them time and love, understanding and care, they make very close companions who enjoy sharing their lives with us. We should afford them respect, not make life more upsetting and unpleasant for them by punishing them rather than thinking through sensitive

1. Araminta, a cross between a Chinchilla and a spotted tabby, combines the soft gentleness of the Chinchilla with the wildness of spots and stripes. Her character shows the same dichotomy.

2. (top) Sady, a long-haired black cat inherited by Caryll and Kit with their cottage. Now being loved and fed regularly for the first time, she hardly lets her new owners out of her sight.

2. (bottom) Mau, a chocolate Burmese, loves skateboarding.

3. Lucy's cats: Leo, the tabby point Siamese, Max, a Foreign black, and Rupert, a blue point Siamese.

4. Jessica with Jaco, who loves being carried around on people's backs.

5. Missy, a tabby and white who was a semi-wild farm kitten before she came to live with Caryll, Kit and Toby. Her early life has left her with an innate wariness of people, but she is as loving as her fear will allow her.

6. Jaco plays in the garden with Matthew – a joyous *pas de deux* born of mutual trust and affection.

7. Missy may be shy, but she is never too nervous to ask for cheese.

8. The goddess and her acolyte. Folly, Lecia's lilac Burmese, greeting Bast.

ways of dealing with behaviour problems. There are several tactics by which a cat's behaviour can be modified, none of which need involve punishment.

So why do people punish their pets, thereby causing both pain and physical and mental damage? If you find yourself making a habit of such treatment, you should certainly take a look at your own emotional make-up. Very occasionally we may all lose our temper with our animal companions, but so long as it does not happen often and we do not hurt them, they appear none the worse. This is different from punishing your cat, causing it pain and anxiety, or being overly strict with it, expecting it to conform to rules and regulations that it may not understand or which are totally unreasonable. As so often is the case, this urge to punish may have been ingrained by childhood experiences, and it may help you to understand how this can happen if we look at the upbringing of a man whom I shall call Mr Carstairs.

Mr Carstairs was the only child born to a couple late in their lives. His parents had very rigid views on life, probably the result of their own emotional insecurity. Dinner was always at a set time, indeed the whole house was run to a strict routine. In this framework the family functioned and life proceeded relatively peacefully although somewhat restrictedly.

In order to achieve this ordered existence, rules had to be made, and if you have rules they must be enforced. The obvious way of doing this was by punishment. If they had tried to implement the rules by understanding and discussion, although that would have given the same degree of security, it would have allowed for rules to be occasionally altered or broken, causing the parents to feel out of control and fearful.

So Mr Carstairs was taught that security means rules: this is the way to survive; and his life took on a strict uniformity. When he finally left home, having failed to break away from his parents' image, he was doomed to choose a wife who was excessively neat and tidy, a garden where flowers grew in straight lines and a car that had to be washed every Sunday.

If Mr Carstairs had any pets that he projected onto, they would also have to conform to the rules or incur punishment. It might not even occur to him that the pet might have a problem understanding the rules, and because of this might suffer greatly. It would be likely that Mr Carstairs would have a dog rather than a cat, as dogs are more willing to be controlled by their owners; their personalities and their desire to be themselves are more easily suppressed, thus making Mr Carstairs feel in control of life.

Mr Carstairs is just a straightforward example of a person living a rather narrow and restricted life and inflicting it on all those he projects onto, whilst believing he is doing it for their own welfare.

It can also happen that when people are taught a strict moral code, which is enforced not by understanding but by punishment, the degree to which they punish those they project onto may be governed by their own fears about themselves. If they feel out of control emotionally, the chances are that they will be stricter and punish those close

to them more often. The problem is made worse by the
fact that if they unreasonably restrict themselves through
fear, they are much more likely to have perverse thoughts
that seem to arise out of nowhere, making them feel even
more out of control. Then they persecute the person or
animal they project onto even more frequently.

8 Cruelty to Cats

There are numerous reasons why people are cruel to
animals and I can only suggest a few here. Where
possible it is these people's own psyches that should
be healed. I have said before that how we treat people
and animals is an indication of the condition of our own
minds. Unfortunately there are those who persecute cats
because they are unable to come to terms with what the
cat may symbolise (such as feminine qualities, mystery or
selfcontainedness). In order to alleviate these problems
they hurt the poor cat.

People brought up in a hostile environment, with a
predominantly negative animus or anima, will have a
negative unconscious image of themselves. They will
view the world and its inhabitants as hostile. Feeling
continually afraid, and with violence the only means they
know of dealing with fear, they may cause an animal a
great deal of suffering.

For people cut off from their feelings because of
negative experiences, and with few or no examples of

love and respect to guide them, it is possible that they will actually use cruelty as a way of experiencing emotion. This is because fear and pain are very powerful feelings, and being cruel to the victim they project onto allows the persecutors to experience both of these vicariously, without suffering themselves.

The other obvious reason is power. If through being bullied or dominated a person suffers humiliation and a lack of self-worth, he will seek to obtain power and dominance over weaker creatures by means of violence. This reassures him that he is still in control. Children may try to bully and dominate each other in order to achieve self-confidence; young men may bully others to clarify their sexuality and masculinity, and the more insecure they feel the more they may need to find reassurance through violence. If they are not physically large enough or strong enough to dominate other boys, they may choose weaker victims, including animals. It is often the boys whose fathers are themselves very macho, who develop this nasty attitude. They cannot live up to the father's overpowering image, and so feel insecure about their own masculinity.

Cultural factors are also responsible for the suffering inflicted on many cats. Ideas about the way cats should be treated have been passed on through generation after generation, only being changed by free-thinking people who are able to break the pattern. Farmers are an example of this: they used to believe, and some still do, that a hungry cat catches more mice. This is a fallacy. A well-fed cat is fitter, has more energy and is bigger and heavy enough to handle large rodents. Thankfully, due to some thoughtful people and bright children who do not blindly follow tradition, many farms are now changing and taking responsibility for the well-being of their cats, to the mutual benefit of cats and farmer.

This brings us to what is probably the most common form of cruelty to cats: cruelty through ignorance. Education can be the remedy here. Ideally schools should include a detailed programme for children on the welfare of pets. I know much has been written on the subject, but this relies on the willingness of parents or children to read those books. A project at school, however, would be very informative and would educate the children whom books fail to reach. Unfortunately, with increasing emphasis being placed in schools on academic qualifications, there

will be less time for equipping children to live in a more humane and caring society. I am sure that thoughtful teachers, who realise that tomorrow's society will be made up of today's children, will do all they can to educate their pupils in the fullest sense of the word, but they can only do so much in the time available.

I am never sure whether it is ignorance or selfishness that leads parents to allow their children to maul and pull at animals. Not much common sense is needed to understand that a small animal can be easily hurt in the hands of young children who are not always aware of their own strength. We all know, from our first knock or graze, that we feel pain if damaged. How is it, then, that these parents do not realise, or do not want to recognise, that animals feel pain too?

I did hear of one parent who allowed her small children to take a baby rabbit to bed. The children were so rough with the rabbit, not realising the sensitivity needed to handle a live animal as against a toy, that it died. Cats, being small animals, are often subjected to this unthinking kind of cruelty, and if a kitten scratches a child in order to defend itself it is then punished or thrown out. There must be an element of callous stupidity in such treatment, coupled with a complete lack of imagination.

Cruelty through neglect is very common, sometimes arising because people are unable to get in touch with their inner feelings, and cannot project love and compassion; their whole attitude to life is materialistic. When an animal no longer suits their specific purpose, it is neglected. This type of person can at least be helped to achieve a more positive self-image, with the concern for others that goes with it.

Selfishness is certainly one reason why people may be blind to the needs of their pets and the responsibilities of a two-way relationship; all they desire is to fulfil their own needs. This is a dangerous philosophy, for to cause pain and suffering to any living creature from purely selfish motives is to throw their own psyche out of balance. It cannot bring mental or physical peace.

Pain can also be caused to those we project onto as a means to test our own strengths. You see this commonly in father-and-son situations. A father expecting his son to be a man – not showing emotion, putting up with physical pain and enduring all kinds of manly pursuits – is thus reassured that he himself is strong, and he is prepared to see his son suffer in order to obtain this assurance. It can also be seen in the man who projects onto his aggressive dog and encourages it to fight in the hope that it will win. This gives the owner some sort of misplaced pride in his own masculinity.

Often a tom cat will not be neutered so that the owner can revel in the cat's sexual conquests as if they reflected on himself. What really happens is that the un-neutered cat fathers many kittens, which in turn are killed or abandoned. The tom cat's owner overlooks this in order to obtain some form of personal gratification.

There are areas of human nature which are not yet understood. Hundreds of cases of cruelty seem to have no reason and defy explanation. It appears that humans have an innate potential to be cruel and selfish, just as they also have the ability to love. This, however, does not excuse our diabolical behaviour to our fellow animals. It is argued that humans have the ability to choose and decide what actions to take; if this is the case, why do we still choose to hurt and persecute animals? Perhaps as we understand more about human nature, and people are made more aware of animals' suffering, things will improve. Taking responsibility for our own actions would help, and being aware that we have a choice to create an environment that can be enjoyed and shared by all living things.

9 Neurosis

Another, less obvious, and fairly rare way you may misuse your cat arises through neurosis, although over-protected cats generally lead happier lives than those misused through neglect or ill-treatment. Over-protection is not a perfect situation, but at least the cat is safe, well-fed and loved. Whenever a cat is restricted through your own neurosis this signals a lack of peace and harmony within you, the owner.

If you are feeling well-adjusted and content, you will give your cat respect and consideration. If, on the other hand, you are beset by anxieties, your problems will filter through to affect the cat's life. When you view life through a negative self-image, formed by negative events and a predominantly negative animus or anima, you see it as a frightening experience. And by projecting your fears onto your cat you may become more and more protective towards your pet, until your attitude reaches a point at which it becomes a neurosis. The higher your inner fences become, the more restrictions you place on your cat.

I am not referring here to restrictions which are based on sound reasoning and common sense, such as keeping your cat indoors when living near busy roads, or near dangerous situations like building sites. If cats have been reported missing or injured in your area, or if your cat is inclined to climb in through open car windows, it is only sensible to keep him inside. Whenever there is a marked increase in the stealing of cats the owner should be particularly vigilant. An owner who has projected strongly onto a cat and formed a strong bond with it is bound to suffer very acutely if it is stolen. In any case, keeping your cat in at night remains the only wise policy, since more cats are killed, injured or go missing at night than at any other time. All these are eminently reasonable restrictions, although some people are only too ready to label you neurotic. However, beyond this lies a grey area of subtle, vague and irrational fears which may lead to quite unreasonable restrictions being placed upon your pet.

Sometimes a husband will ridicule and persecute his wife for being over-protective about their cat, even to the point of making her life a misery. This tends to make the situation worse when her anxieties arise from a negative self-image, and by presenting a negative image to his partner the husband is only reinforcing and perpetuating the neurosis. What she really needs is to be given love and support which presents her with a positive image of herself.

Negative projection and the resulting neurosis can take dramatic forms. One of the most startling cases I have heard of came to me through two close friends, Bob and Judy, who told me about their friend Jane. Apparently she had a very negative childhood, so it was not surprising that she should have developed problems in adult life. Married but childless, she naturally projected strongly onto her pets, an un-neutered tom cat and two Dobermann Pinschers. The cat was left entire because Jane felt that neutering was cruel, and she kept him indoors all the time so that he would be safe. The combination of these two factors drove the poor cat almost out of his mind: with his instinct to mate still intact, he spent most of his time looking for ways to get outside. He also sprayed the house with his scent until the smell was almost overpowering, although Jane seemed impervious to this. Her own fears were so strong that they affected all her decisions, and in the process the cat and his needs were completely submerged and lost.

The dogs, being nervous and dominant, were awkward to approach, and any person visiting the house had to conform to a set procedure. Bob and Judy were invited to tea one day, and were to experience this problem at first hand. They were told to stay in the lounge while the dogs were in the kitchen, and after Jane had given them tea and biscuits the dogs were allowed into the lounge to meet the visitors, who had been warned not to move. Jane had told them that whatever happened, they mustn't stand up when the dogs were in the room because if they got much above the animals' eye level they might be mistaken for the vet, and then they would very likely get bitten.

Feeling rather nervous, Bob and Judy sat there as the dogs entered. One of them came over to Judy and proceeded to eat her biscuit, and since she dared not move, she had to sit there and watch this happening. Jane interpreted this as a good sign: the dog obviously liked Judy. Next came the problem of how to reach the tea-table. Jane's solution was that Bob and Judy should slip out of their armchairs and creep along in a crouching position to the tea-table, where they could slide onto the dining chairs. This they managed to do, and they got tea safely over with Bob and Judy still in one piece.

Then Bob was asked if he would go out into the garden as Jane wanted a photograph of one of the dogs. Once in the garden, she explained that the photograph would require the dog to be off the lead. She also asked Bob to throw a ball into the air so that a picture could be taken of the dog jumping. She duly let the dog off the lead, whereupon it made straight for Bob who ran off towards the fence and vaulted over it. Once safely over, his voice could be heard asking, 'Can I throw it from here?'

It is quite clear that although Jane had some elaborate stories to explain why the animals behaved as they did, her own anxieties and dependence on them influenced the way she treated them, and although she did not realise it, they were reacting to this. Had she been aware of what was happening, perhaps she might have been able to seek help, so making life for herself, the animals and her husband much easier.

The plight of another childless couple was even sadder. Their affection was lavished on two pedigree kittens, and with the husband away much of the time on business, the cats became his wife's closest companions.

All went well until they had to go away for a couple of weeks to visit their family. The cats were boarded in a cattery, and on their return they were very distressed to find one of the animals in poor health. It did not seem to respond to treatment, and both partners became increasingly worried about it. While it was ill, additional business and family problems began to cause them further concern, so that the accumulation of anxiety eventually told on the wife particularly. She unknowingly projected her anxieties onto the cats, becoming more and more neurotic about their health and well-being, until eventually she refused to let them out of her sight, afraid to go away in case something happened to them. Even after the sick cat had recovered, she could not bring herself to accept the offer of kind friends to take care of them in her absence.

I think that anyone who has ever owned a cat will sympathise with this woman. Trapped by her own mounting anxiety, she allowed her life to be ruled by her neurosis, unable to see that her personal problems were intensifying her unconscious fears for her cats. She desperately needed someone to help her separate her worries from her natural concern for the cats' welfare, and realise that by projecting her anxieties onto them she was actually restricting herself and them.

From these two stories it is easy to see how a vicious circle can arise if you are unaware of your emotional state and its consequences. So if you notice that you are becoming neurotic about the welfare of your cat, you should take a look at your own life and try to understand your own inner fears and anxieties. These are what you are projecting onto your cat, and as you come to terms with them your new reassurance will also be projected onto your cat. This, combined with a more objective self-awareness, will enable you to treat your cat as an individual in its own right.

10 Taking in Stray Cats, and Caring for Cats in Distress

People who feel a compulsion to take in and care for stray cats may be responding to the animals' distress because they themselves feel unhappy or deprived in some way; they are projecting this onto the cats which symbolise and remind them of their own needs. In the nurturing and caring that follows they are unconsciously trying to heal themselves, and caring about the well-being of their cats will be of positive benefit to them. As the cat responds, so will the person caring for it, so that the whole process helps both cat and owner. Other people, having themselves suffered in various ways, are able to empathise with animals in need, and to work hard to alleviate their pain and discomfort. These people have a kind and caring attitude developed through their own experience.

As in cases of cruelty to animals, when we look at those who devote their lives to alleviating pain and suffering, it is not always possible to explain their motivation. All one can say is that some people seem to have a natural affinity with animals, and an innate benevolence which leads them to work with single-minded dedication in their efforts to prevent any unnecessary suffering. These people deserve all the support and admiration we can give them. They are trying to make the world a richer place to live in, and for that we should all be grateful.

I have given only a few examples of the ways in which we may treat our cats, but the range of possibilities here is very wide. In particular, the reasons for ill-treatment are so many and varied that it is difficult to be too specific without studying individual cases. However, one general principle emerges clearly: if a person projects his or her negative feelings onto animals, or is incapable of projecting love and respect, this can result in dire consequences for the animal kingdom. If any of you are aware that you are ill-treating your pet, it is your own unconscious self-image which should be examined.

Finally, a word on behalf of the cats which receive such a variety of treatment – good and bad – from human beings. It is not widely recognised that the cat's IQ is extremely high compared to most other animals'. Those who still doubt its intelligence would be well advised to read *Incredible Cats* by David Greene, an experimental psychologist who has researched the extraordinary abilities and powers of cats, and the ways in which they benefit human beings. He concludes:

> The fact is that most cats are extremely bright, possessing an IQ which is, in many ways, far superior to that of dogs and surpassed in the animal kingdom only by man's closest relatives, monkeys and chimps.

Once you are aware of the high intelligence of cats, you can understand that their suffering when ill-treated or abandoned must be far greater than has been generally realised. If this were more widely appreciated, perhaps that knowledge might in itself act as a deterrent. The term 'dumb animal' has had a very damaging effect, since it suggests that animals are devoid of mind and soul and can therefore be exploited by us for our own needs. Equally destructive is the view that animals were put on earth specifically for our use, giving us *carte blanche* to treat them as we please. These are very dangerous ideas, leading not only to animal abuse and suffering, but ultimately to ecological imbalance on our planet.

An animal has its own form of consciousness, its own awareness of things. Its view of life may be somewhat different from ours, but both animals and humans can think and feel. Suffering is an experience which is common to us all, and a cat – or indeed any pet – is not a plaything to be toyed with and then discarded. Pets abandoned after being given love and comfort feel totally baffled, hurt and bewildered by the experience. I believe that the more we are aware of this capacity for suffering the less likely we shall be to abandon them.

In the end it comes down to this: if animals are perceived as feeling and thinking beings in their own right, perhaps we can relate to them more profoundly and act with a greater respect for their needs. In the depth of that new relationship we may begin to see them, not as inferior beings, but as they really are. I came across the following words by Henry Beeston, in his book *The Outermost House*, which I feel sum it up superbly:

We need another and a wiser and perhaps a more mystical concept of animals. We patronise them for their incompleteness, for their tragic fate of having taken form so far below ourselves. And therein we err and greatly err. For the animal shall not be measured by man. In a world more complete than ours, with extensions of the senses we have lost or never attained, living by voices we shall never hear, they are not brethren, they are not underlings: they are other nations, caught with ourselves in the net of life and time, fellow prisoners of that splendour and travail of the earth.

6

Instinctive Sympathy

When you are in the company of other people, to a certain degree you will find yourself picking up their feelings. We have all experienced a positive feeling in the company of positive people, and a negative feeling when others are in a negative mood. You may automatically sense the thoughts, feelings and emotions of others who are with you, and sometimes you may think that these originate in you rather than someone else, and may mistake them for your own feelings. This can be even stronger with people close to you.

Animals are also capable of sensing your feelings and reacting to them, and again this effect will be stronger when they are close to you. Exactly how the process works is not fully understood. Perhaps body language plays a part, since both animals and humans are able to interpret very subtle signals. However, this does not account for the occasions when the person or animal concerned is out of sight. This process of sensitivity and reaction to others' feelings may be regarded as being in sympathy with them. Because it takes place below the level of the reasoning consciousness, I use the term 'instinctive sympathy' when I refer to it.

To make it clearer, we need to take a brief look at the importance of the ego in relation to this process. If, through a weak ego, your awareness of yourself as an individual is poorly developed, you are more vulnerable to the influence of other people's feelings. This also leaves you closer to the power of the unconscious, in which dwell the instincts, archetypes, anima and animus. Of course you should listen to the unconscious – it is very important to do so – but a weak ego is in danger of being overpowered by it.

People with a dominant ego have their own set of problems, such as feeling so separate from all other life forms that they are unable to relate to others, or to pick up other people's feelings easily. They may also be deaf to their own instincts, which means that the instincts may manifest themselves in a most unpleasant way.

If you are lucky enough to have a balanced ego, it gives you a realistic view of life and a greater chance of accepting your instincts, without being overpowered by them. It also enables you to be sensitive to other people's feelings without being completely influenced by them.

To help you understand why your cat may be vulnerable to your influence, let's try to imagine what might be going on in its mind.

Until fairly recently this subject was rather neglected,

because psychologists thought that animals were just instinctually functioning beings, lacking any process of thought. Valerie O'Farrell describes this well in her book *Manual of Canine Behaviour*:

It has been assumed that, below the level of primates, an animal responds automatically, without conscious reflection, on the basis of associative learning; that its responses are habitual, built up from past experience, and that its consciousness is rather like that of a car driver who drives without thinking and arrives at his destination without any idea of how he got there. To put it another way, it was assumed that Pavlov's dogs, which learned to salivate at the sound of a bell when the bell had been frequently paired with food, did so automatically and unconsciously without formulating any expectations or theories, such as 'The bell means food' . . .

On the other hand, recent research in the learning theory tradition has produced findings which can only be explained by postulating that animals do after all have expectations and formulate theories (Mackintosh, 1974). There is also plenty of other evidence that animals and, more specifically, dogs do more than just automatically associate stimuli and response . . . It has also been shown that wolves have 'mental maps' of their territory. They find their way from one place to another by the shortest route, not necessarily a route which they have ever taken before.

In tests cats have shown that they, too, are capable of problem-solving and that they have a high intelligence. I have already referred to David Greene's fascinating book *Incredible Cats*; in it he gives examples of tests carried out at the Wesleyan University in Connecticut by Dr Donald Adams, one of which involved cats being trained in the laboratory to pull a box on wheels around the room. After a while he suspended pieces of food from the ceiling on a long string. The box was placed a few feet away from the food and a female cat was then brought into the room. After a few unsuccessful attempts to grab the food by standing on the box and reaching over, or by jumping at it from the floor, she decided to stop and think it through. Cats often have a thinking spot, where they will sit and groom or stare into space while they ponder and apparently put the world to rights. This cat sat and groomed herself for a while, but she must have been busily thinking all the time. Suddenly she stopped in mid-wash, stared at the food, then ran to the box and pulled it until it was directly under the food. Then, jumping onto the box, she reached up for the food, detached it from the string and settled down to enjoy it. By using reason and intellect she had obtained her treat.

The cats I have known have had no great problem in learning how to open the fridge, and my first two Siamese did this frequently. So when I visited a family of Siamese cats and kittens, hoping to buy a kitten for myself, I was not surprised to see the kitchen barricaded. The fridge had a chair wedged against it, to prevent the cats opening it, and the cupboard doors were tied together with rope. The drawers, however, were left defenceless, and one of the Siamese had opened them – much to the delight of the kittens who were jumping in and out.

Working as a pair, my Burmese kitten and his mother are quite capable of opening room doors. The kitten jumps up, puts his paws together each side of the door handle and uses his weight to release the catch, while his mother sits below and pulls the door open with her paw.

William, my red point Siamese, used to retrieve his sheepskin ball. I would throw it several times in the same direction between two chairs, and then at random I would throw it in a slightly different direction, making it land out of sight behind one of the chairs. He would run off in the same direction as before, see that the ball was not there, think for a moment or two and then move off round the chair, landing on the ball straight away; he had obviously reasoned it out.

Bessle, one of the Burmese kittens I mentioned in Chapter 4, which now belongs to Norma and Fred, is exceptionally bright and entertains her owners with displays of her intelligence. One of her favourite toys is a string of beads which hangs on a hook on the wall. On one occasion, her sister Be-Be wanted to get them down. She tugged at the beads, found they would not dislodge, lost interest and left them alone. Bessle, who had been watching, then approached the beads and also tugged at them. They did not move. She sat back, summed up the situation, jumped up onto a nearby shelf and lifted the beads with her paw, up and off the hook.

Other animals also give evidence of high intelligence. Whales and dolphins, for instance, have intricate communication systems; but while they seem able to understand at least a part of our language, we are a long way from being able to understand any of theirs. Many animals learn to respond to our spoken words, far more readily than we can master their methods of communication.

Cats seem able to sense disasters before they happen. They have been reported as showing awareness of impending earthquakes or tornadoes before any human could sense them, and without the use of electronic equipment. I have even read of one cat which warned its owner of an unexploded bomb. They are also renowned for their ability to find their way home over long distances, and even to find owners who have moved to a new district.

The tests carried out by Dr Adams and many other psychologists, and the observations of people who have lived in the company of cats, seem to prove beyond doubt that cats have a reasoning mind. There is a basic similarity in the psychological make-up of the cat and ourselves, but although we now credit it with a certain amount of intelligence, we can only measure its intellect against our own. Man tends to assess all animals in terms of himself, and when they do not match up, he feels that he is superior and can therefore use and control them. If cats measured man against themselves, there is no doubt that he would be found wanting in their eyes, too. We need to develop a more balanced perception, and realise that we are just one of many species that share this planet, all depending on each other to survive, all equally worthy of respect.

Cats have an admirable completeness, a sensory ability that we may never fully know or understand; but even so, it is hard for us to tell how aware they are of their own individuality. Do they have a sense of who and what they are? Some would argue that this is impossible, but as we have seen, having rigid opinions about cats' psychology can lead to a very narrow view of them, one which we are already having to alter in the light of new evidence.

Although much has been written on modifying your cat's behaviour by the way you treat it, and tests have shown that the theories work successfully in practice, little is known (except by cat owners) of how a cat's behaviour is affected by the more subtle signals it receives through being 'in sympathy' with its owner's feelings.

You react without being aware of it to your cat's moods. A depressed cat makes your spirits sink, a happy cat makes you feel good. The reason for this may be that if your cat is happy it reassures you that you are taking care of it both physically and emotionally. Equally, if the cat is depressed you will feel that you have somehow been neglectful in your relationship with it; you may worry that it might be unwell. Conversely, people who are close to their cats say that their pets are able to detect their moods. Perhaps their happiness reassures the cat that everything is fine, just as their bad moods make the cat feel more anxious.

Either way, the consequences are the same: if you are happy, the chances are that your cat will feel happy; if you are depressed or irritable, your cat may also feel upset. Either of you may influence the other's state of mind.

The basic independent nature of cats seems to save most of them from being overly reactive to our feelings; dogs do not have this protection and are more susceptible to the influence of instinctive sympathy. This is perhaps because dogs, as pack animals, are by nature more alert to our moods; conforming to the commands of the leader is very important to them. If the leader is displeased they may get a nasty bite – it's enough to make anyone more susceptive!

A kitten born in the wild may never fully respond to people. It will accept your food and the comfort of your home, but it may never lose its natural self-preservation instinct which makes it nervous and wary of people. Such a cat, along with those which have had insecure kittenhoods, or have experienced a traumatic event in their lives, or who simply have a nervous personality, are more likely to be sensitive to others' anxieties, as they see and feel all of life as threatening. They are more adept at picking up others' stresses since a stressful animal or human is a potential danger to them.

A cat which has had a secure kittenhood and a reasonably happy life is more likely to be self-confident and so less affected by the emotions of others. This is not to say that such cats are insensitive to our negative feelings. The confidence they have acquired through being exposed to people from an early age, and always feeling safe and contented, will tend to make them more responsive to our moods but less disturbed by our negative emotions.

Although we domesticate cats, they still live part of their lives as wild cats. But if you establish a close relationship with your cat by giving it your time and attention, it will be more likely to respond to you. Each of you will project onto the other and your lives will become entangled as you develop a sensitivity to one another's moods. Certainly a number of pedigree breeds, including Siamese and Burmese cats, enjoy the company of their human companions and have a keen ability to sense and react to our feelings. They also display a higher level of intelligence than the average cat: perhaps a history of close contact with human beings who have lavished attention on them has released more of their potential.

Cats may become withdrawn if they feel insecure and

frightened, and may lead their own lives more intensely. The extent to which a cat can walk alone and deal with its anxiety in its own undramatic way does mean that problems of this nature are much more likely to be overlooked in cats than in dogs. If your neurotic dog starts snarling at – or biting – visitors, you should clearly take some action. If your neurotic cat withdraws into itself and walks alone, the problem can mount up over a long period without your being aware of it. The cat's tendency to aloofness, and its basic independence, are mirrors and symbols of the unconscious – something hidden and unseen which you can never fully know or control.

Cats can of course become aggressive if they are insecure and frightened, particularly if they are cornered or harassed while they are in an anxious state. They can express their aggression in various ways, sometimes even biting or scratching their owners if they are exceptionally anxious, even if the owner has done nothing to provoke an attack. This reaction – not unlike a human one – is simply discharging energy on the nearest suitable subject, and is also the cat's way of protecting itself while it feels vulnerable.

In his book *Understanding Your Cat*, Michael W. Fox gives examples of aggressive behaviour in cats. An unhappy and aggressive female cat which had killed her own kittens was brought to Professors Blin and Faveau of the Alfort Veterinary College in Paris. Before she developed this bad-tempered behaviour she had been the centre of attention and delighted in being cuddled.

It was discovered that she had changed once her owners started to show affection to some of her earlier offspring. This led her to become depressed; she went off her food, neglected to groom herself and became difficult to handle. In her unkempt state, with her uncertain temper, she did not invite attention, and so she became more and more unhappy. Once the family realised how rejected she was feeling, and how much she needed to be made a fuss of, they did all they could to make her feel loved and wanted. Within a few days she was well and happy again. Fox also describes a cat which expressed its unhappiness at the death of its master by becoming aggressive towards other members of the household.

You should remember, too, that if you yourself are anxious, your attitude to your cat and your treatment of it may have changed, causing it to become uncertain and insecure. In some cases cats may betray their anxiety by soiling areas other than their litter trays, refusing to eat, or displaying other forms of abnormal behaviour. Even if anxiety is the most likely cause, a cat which develops any of these habits should be thoroughly checked by a vet, as ill-health can easily produce the same symptoms. Once you have eliminated physical problems, you should then look for any obvious reason to account for your cat's sudden anxiety, such as a new pet or the arrival of a new baby, teasing by children or harassment from another cat which has moved into your neighbourhood – perhaps your cat feels that its territory is under threat. Have you recently moved house? Or is your cat lonely and in need of more attention? I heard of one woman who had several cats, all very close to her, which started soiling when she suffered a bereavement; as she recovered, so did her cats.

If, after checking thoroughly, you can find no reason for your cat's abnormal behaviour, it is probable that it is picking up your own anxieties and reacting to them.

Anxiety can also affect the physical welfare of your cat: it is likely to lower its resistance to disease. If cats are ill and need nursing, they become very sensitive to their owner's feelings, and since they can become very depressed when they are ill, it is beneficial for a sick cat to have an owner with a positive and caring attitude. Indeed, such people stand a better chance of having a well-adjusted and healthy cat. This is not just because of instinctive sympathy, but because the owners are less likely to use their animals as a focus for their emotions, or to behave inconsistently towards them.

Carole C. Wilbourn, a cat therapist in America, gives many examples of anxiety in cats in her book *Cat Talk*, and I recommend this book as very interesting reading. She writes about the sensitivity of her own cats to her emotions:

> Sometimes a person's anxiety can affect their cat's peace of mind. I have definitely found that Sam and Baggins are very sensitive to my anxious moods. If I return home with a lot on my mind, no time to spare, and less time to spend with them, they waste little time in letting me know that they are upset.

She goes on to describe a sick and extremely aggressive cat named Cary which she was treating, whose life had been very traumatic:

> Cary was so vulnerable to anxiety, I thought it was necessary to keep him in a separate room and to supervise his visits. I provided him with almost constant nursing care by nurses whose energy level did not threaten him. Most of Cary's day would be spent in a comfortable lap. His exquisite ability to let his body relax completely and 'breathe in' love and attention was as powerful as his ability to attack when he felt threatened. Thus, Cary was an incredible barometer of tension. His ability to empathise was great when it came to being aware of just how relaxed the possessor of any particular lap was. I remember one time he sat in my lap and started to swish his tail and glare at me. At first I was confused and even apprehensive; then I realised I was tense. It wasn't until I relaxed both my mind and body that Cary relaxed and curled up in my lap.

From this example, you can see that by watching your cats' reactions you can to some degree learn about yourself.

Sometimes a cat will display an obvious dislike of men. The classic explanation would be to suggest that the cat has at some time been ill-treated by a man, or else that it sees the man as a threat to its territory. It may even attack or threaten the man, although it is more likely that a dog would react in this territorial way. This is partly due to the fact that a cat is usually allowed freedom to move about out of doors and is able to establish a 'pecking order' with other cats. Sometimes, if a cat feels its territory is under threat by another animal or person, it may demonstrate its anxiety by marking its territory with faeces and urine – and sometimes this includes the house. Wild cats mark the edge of their territories by leaving excrement exposed. Perhaps the cat will react to its territory – that is, your home – being violated by intruders by spraying their belongings. It may also temporarily go off its food, and in extreme cases leave home.

Of course jealousy, as we saw earlier, may be the cause of the cat's aggression, and in the case of a friend of mine this does appear to have been so. She had a household full of cats, and devoted a great deal of time to them; she would often walk about with one of them draped round her neck. This was fine until her man friend came close to her, when the cat around her neck would hiss and swipe at him. Another friend once had a very nervous cat which was afraid of a man because of the vibration of his rather large feet.

However, there is also the possibility that a cat's dislike of men could stem from instinctive sympathy. Although the owner might not be aware of her own fear of men, this fear could still be powerful enough for the cat to detect it and react in sympathy. If the routine is repeated often enough the cat will soon associate men with fear. Now while I do not dispute the validity of the previous explanations – and in many cases they may be correct –

I believe it is also true that instinctive sympathy can be a very real alternative. So if you own a cat which is afraid of men, and you are unable to find any other explanation, perhaps you should consider instinctive sympathy and try to examine your own unconscious fears.

In a close relationship with a human being, a cat may pick up and reflect the most surprising aspects of its owner's character. My friend Lucy has two Siamese cats, Rupert and Leo, which she bought for herself and her younger son, Charles. Rupert arrived first and became her cat, with a very close bond between them, while Leo attached himself to Charles. Rupert is a blue point Siamese male of extraordinary beauty. Lucy is a very attractive, intelligent woman, with blue-grey hair and clear blue eyes, so she naturally thinks Rupert is the most beautiful cat in the whole world – an opinion shared wholeheartedly by Rupert himself!

The one big difference in their respective appearances – apart from the obvious fact that Rupert is a cat and Lucy is a human being – is that Rupert is very slim, with long, elegant legs, while Lucy is overweight. This has been one of her biggest headaches for many a year. Throughout her youth she was very slender, but as the years went by, two children and difficult circumstances took their toll, and Lucy developed a compulsion to eat as a compensation for the problems that faced her. Not long after coming to live with her, Rupert also decided that food was one of his most important priorities. Lucy had a sophisticated taste in food, and so of course did Rupert. When in Lucy's company he would eat only the best, but while staying with me in my cattery he would down any cat food with relish. At home he would not touch cat food until every other possibility had been explored. His desire to eat made him bully Leo from his dish, and here Lucy's reaction was very firm. Because of the battle she had been waging with herself, she saw the need to discipline Rupert, feeling very strongly about his weakness. She now goes to great lengths to make sure he remains his elegant self, and does not allow him to dominate Leo at feeding time. The battle outside herself, which is really a reflection of the battle within, is being played out.

This is not the first animal with which Lucy has had to fight this battle: her dog Heather also desired food more than any other dog I have ever known. Although Heather's gluttony did not develop into Rupert's refined taste, throughout the dog's life Lucy faced the same struggle that she is now facing with Rupert – and of course with herself.

Rupert's compulsion to eat may be part of his personality, or it may be due to his early experiences as a young kitten. Or Lucy's own addiction may have influenced his eating pattern, if she inadvertently adopted a feeding routine with him that represented her own needs. But it is possible that Rupert picks up subtle feelings and messages from Lucy.

Leo, the other cat in Lucy's life, was bought partly as company for Rupert and partly because she felt that her son Charles would benefit from a cat of his own. Leo is a seal tabby point male Siamese, and Lucy was delighted with him: he was small and always looked like a kitten, a perfect companion for Charles. He also fulfilled Lucy's need to feel comforted by his kittenish (childlike) appearance. With her sons growing rapidly she could still keep some of their childlike image in Leo.

Leo and Charlie quickly became great friends, and very soon we began to notice a similarity between them. Charlie is a child who tends to throw himself down with a thud wherever he wants to sit, and Leo quickly developed this trait. Coming onto your lap he would just thump down, with none of the treading around which cats usually do, turning a few times as if to say, 'Shall I lie this way or that?' Charles is a great seeker of comfort, and one thing a cat really knows about is how to find comfort; I have often thought that it may be this that attracts him to cats.

I know that my friends Lecia and Peter look back with a smile at the episode in their lives I am going to describe to you, but I am sure that they did not find it so funny at the time. It was so odd, however, that I feel what happened was surely more than mere coincidence.

Lecia and Peter live a very conventional, happy, and well ordered life. Lecia has been a lifelong fan of animals, taking a keen interest in all wildlife, with an overwhelming passion for cats.

We met some six years ago, after seeing each other frequently in the doctor's and the vet's waiting rooms. It turned out that we both suffered from the same health problem and both had elderly Siamese cats, and after researching their pedigrees, we found the cats were closely related. People often remarked that we even looked alike. We developed a close friendship, each supporting the other through the deaths of our beloved Siamese.

Lecia adored Burmese cats as well as Siamese, and after the death of her first Burmese she decided to buy a new kitten. She chose a lilac female, and aptly named her Folly. Not long afterwards she decided to get another kitten to keep Folly company, and bought a pretty lilac tabby point Siamese which she named Peri. Poor Peri never really enjoyed good health and required frequent visits to the vet. Lecia spent many an hour both in the vet's and the doctor's, as her own health was still giving her trouble.

One dreadful evening Peri returned home with her leg mutilated and it had to be amputated the following day; it was a harrowing time and for a few days her life hung by a thread. We all felt depressed, but within a week it seemed likely that Peri would survive: she had already started to try walking on her three legs, a task she tackled and conquered with remarkable speed. She was given lots of love and support and slowly resumed as near normal a life as possible, apart from a pronounced limp.

Then one day Folly the Burmese, who is very close to Peter, also appeared with a limp. She had jumped down from a height and had badly sprained her leg; this did not heal properly for over a year. So now both cats were limping.

Normally I have noticed that cats appear to behave like us, but both Peter and Lecia seem to have developed some instinctive sympathy with their cats, because Peter, who had had a grumbling knee for many years, suddenly found that it had become a very bad-tempered knee, causing him a great deal of pain. Out of the household of four, three were now limping. Not long afterwards, Lecia sprained her ankle and completed the circle. *All four* were limping at the same time!

Could this be instinctive sympathy carried to the extreme? I shall leave you to make up your own minds.

We should not, however, overlook the beneficial aspects of instinctive sympathy. When your cat reacts to your more positive emotions, the love and affection and joy you transmit to your cat companion is returned to you, strengthening your own capacity to express these emotions, and supporting and nourishing your personality in a most positive way.

7

The Healing Power of Projection

Until quite recently pets were kept well away from hospitals as a matter of definite policy. As a child in a nursing home, one of my greatest desires was to see my dog. If he had been allowed to visit me often, I am sure my heightened spirits would have accelerated my recovery. Now, however, in old people's homes and children's homes – even in prisons – the importance of pets is at last slowly becoming accepted. Indeed, pets have been allowed into some hospitals since the mid 1970s. The loneliness of these institutions is thus being tempered by the warm response of a pet, which helps to promote a sense of well-being and a reassurance of normality.

The cat, with its quiet independence, has proved to be the perfect subject for this type of work; dogs, with their boisterous enthusiasm, can be too overwhelming for some patients. This is particularly important in psychiatric hospitals, where a cat can sometimes be a breakthrough for a patient who has withdrawn from human society and yet is able to reach out and stroke a cat, feeling that the animal is not a threat.

When a patient withdraws from sense stimulation to a large extent, or enters a coma, he has in effect shifted from the conscious world to the unconscious, the symbolic world of the cat. It is here that the cat can sometimes play a remarkable role in therapy. David Greene, in his book *Incredible Cats*, recalls how a ten-year-old Mexican girl, Maria, was brought out of a coma by a cat which constantly licked her fingers. Why this should have succeeded when the efforts of doctors and nurses failed, is not clear. Whilst it is certainly possible that the constant licking of a hand might stimulate brain activity, this does not explain the well-documented success of cats in this type of case when compared with the relative failure of human physiotherapists applying massage. One is led to explore a further fascinating possibility: that the licking process may, in some way we do not at present understand, be able to stimulate the unconscious mind. When this stimulation begins to filter through to the conscious level, there is an increase in brain activity, resulting in the patient's return to consciousness. This explanation would be consistent with the long time-scale involved in such a subtle and complex process: in the case of Maria it took eight days for her to emerge from her coma after the arrival of the cat.

David Greene also describes the case of Billy, an autistic nineteen-year-old who was almost entirely withdrawn into himself. He lay motionless in a hospital bed, staring at a crack on the opposite wall. When Rocky, a cat specially bred to be affectionate and responsive, was placed on his bed, Billy seemed to take no interest in him.

At first Billy had to be coaxed into petting the cat. A nurse would take his hand and move the unresponsive fingers through Rocky's long sleek coat. Gradually, perhaps affected by the animal's obvious enjoyment, Billy began to take an active interest in caressing him and did so without any encouragement. In time he learned to feed, look after and, finally, to play games with the cat.

The breakthrough his doctors had been hoping for came on the day he turned to a nurse and said quietly: 'Rocky's hungry, he wants some food.'

They were the first words he had spoken for more than a decade. From then on progress was swift. A few months afterwards he was well enough to leave hospital and go home to his parents.

Stroking a cat has also been found beneficial for people suffering from high blood pressure: the cat relaxes and purrs, and this has an effect upon the person, relaxing him in turn, so that his blood pressure drops. Because blood pressure can be monitored, it can be seen to be dropping as the person relaxes.

But what of conditions which cannot be monitored so easily? It may reasonably be assumed that if a cat has a relaxing effect on someone suffering from high blood pressure, it can also help in many other stress-related diseases.

In calming and soothing patients who are recovering from strokes and heart attacks, the cat's undemanding but affectionate presence allows the patient to contact the healing within his own unconscious, and releases in him the capacity for relaxation and calmness. As stress is now believed to be a major factor in many types of illness, our cat companions may be of considerable benefit to us. Basically, we project onto the cat, and when the cat relaxes, so do we. Anyone owning a cat will probably already have noticed how its quiet, gentle and meditative nature has a very reassuring and soothing effect.

However, if you cannot communicate with your own feelings you may find it difficult to respond to a cat. I know of one man who simply could not understand the pleasure there is in touching a cat. Even when kittens sat on his lap – a situation which most people find irresistible – he could not respond to them at all. If only he had made an effort to respond to the kittens, they would have responded to him, and he might have experienced the joy of communicating with his own feelings of love and care. I find this situation very sad, for so many people seem locked away in themselves, thinking up all kinds of reasons why they cannot respond to a cat, whilst ignoring the basic underlying problem. In extreme cases this can lead to an almost total exclusion of the emotional experience which is such a vital part of the human condition.

I believe we are only just beginning to explore the possibilities inherent in caressing a cat as a form of emotional therapy. Although this kind of therapy has been used for patients with high blood pressure, its extension into the field of emotional therapy is still in its very earliest stages.

The versatility of the cat as an aid to healing underlines just how remarkably well suited it is for this purpose. It is not too large or overpowering or demanding, since any of these qualities might frighten or deter patients. It is capable of making friendly noises when stroked, can deliver soothing stimuli through licking, and has a coat that is silky and pleasant to touch. The combination of these remarkably attractive and reassuring qualities helps to encourage activity by the patient, and this activity

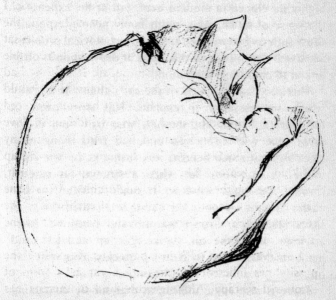

can release pent-up feelings and promote a sense of relaxation and well-being. Where the cat can make a unique contribution is in the use of the sense of touch as a trigger to stimulate brain activity or the flow of emotional energies.

Primitive societies were much more touch-orientated than we are today in many parts of the Western world; the rise of a sophisticated industrialised society has usually been accompanied by a decline in both the use and the acceptability of touch as a means of social interaction. With the development of visual and verbal skills, the senses of sight and hearing have become much more highly developed in modern man, but at the expense of the sense of touch. As a result many people, especially those suffering from some kind of psychological problem, are touch-deprived, and this form of deprivation is often linked to emotional inhibition.

There are some aspects of the cat's ability as a healer which are less easy to explain. This story came to me from a friend. His mother, who had been ill for some time with bronchitis and had tried many remedies without much benefit, was sitting in an arm-chair in her ground-floor flat when a strange cat entered through the open window. It made straight for her chair, climbed up onto her chest, and settled down to sleep. She felt a distinct warmth and easement. After an hour or so the cat awoke, got up and left, and her bronchitis began to clear up quickly from that day on.

There is also some indication that simply contacting

the world of the cat can offer healing in a very subtle yet profound way. This is particularly true for patients who feel trapped by the processes of the conscious mind. Much can be gained by using the Cat Experience as a key to the unconscious, a gateway to liberation into a richer, deeper and fuller area of awareness. Paradoxically, by moving into the Cat Experience, we can also reach an understanding of what it is to become more fully human, for ultimately man is much more than just the rationalising conscious mind. The cat says in effect: 'Stop thinking so much, and start *being* – look at us, we're *being* all the time!'

Viewed in this wider context, as part of a broader relationship which includes healing, the process of give and take between cats and human beings is by no means as one-sided as it might seem, and it is arguable that the cat gives us back full measure for all we give it.

It should not be forgotten, however, that the cat gives freely and without coercion, from a position of independence. The cat is an independent animal by nature, and so an even greater feeling of satisfaction is experienced when it responds to your touch. It is accepting you for what you are, and you don't have to adapt your personality to persuade it to like you. You feel rewarded when cats grace you with their attention. Their demonstrations of a warm and responsive love are given freely and directly without any deviousness or calculation: what they feel, they express. The trustworthiness of their emotional response can enable you to experience a degree of emotional security that is not always available within human relationships. This is partly what makes cats so valuable as companions.

8

Animals as Symbols

Since the age of four I have been devoted to and fascinated by my animal companions. It was at this age that I first demanded to have a dog, and as a result Blackie entered my life; later, when I was eleven, I acquired my first cat, a black and white which I named Whiskey.

In recent years my awareness of a oneness with all living things has increased, partly thanks to my constant cat friends, but also because of a growing realisation that in all of us there is every animal, and in every animal we can find ourselves. The idea of animals as gods, or symbols, therefore seems quite natural.

To understand this concept, you have to realise that the instincts, feelings and emotions which we all possess can be personified as animals. Often the self is symbolised as an animal; it represents our instinctive nature, our joining with all living things, our psyche woven into the whole.

As Aniela Jaffé writes in *Man and his Symbols*:

Even in Christianity, animal symbolism plays a surprisingly great part. Three of the Evangelists have animal emblems: St Luke has the ox, St Mark the lion, and St John the eagle. Only one, St Matthew, is represented as a man or as an angel. Christ himself symbolically appears as the Lamb of God or the fish, but he is also the serpent exalted on the cross, the lion, and in rarer cases the unicorn. These animal attributions of Christ indicate that even the Son of God (the supreme personification of man) can no more dispense with his animal nature than with his higher, spiritual nature. The subhuman as well as the superhuman is felt to belong to the realm of the divine; the relationship of these two aspects of man is beautifully symbolised in the Christmas picture of the birth of Christ, in a stable among animals.

Astrological systems of both East and West offer further examples of animal symbolism. In Western astrology the signs of the Zodiac represent basic aspects of personality. In Chinese astrology each year is assigned to one of twelve animals, such as the Dog, Monkey, Horse or Tiger; and people born in the year of the Monkey, for instance, are said to have strong Monkey attributes in their personality.

The symbolic aspect of animals is seen at its most elaborate in the native American teachings. Some American Indians describe their philosophy of life as a path 'for those who choose to seek Pleasure and Knowledge'. This tradition derives knowledge from all sources – mineral, plant, animal and human – and believes that each animal has its own essence to impart to man. Sun Bear, in his book *The Medicine Wheel Earth Astrology*, describes the four Spirit Keepers of the directions:

South: the Coyote. He teaches survival; he is also the trickster, and tricks you into opening yourself to growth, to learning; even against your will.

West: the Grizzly Bear. Through him we learn our strengths and weaknesses; he also represents introspection and gentle decisions.

North: the Buffalo. His essence is renewal and purity.

East: the Eagle. He flies closest to the sun; he is illumination, wisdom and enlightenment, the connecting link between the human spirit and the Great Spirit.

Two animals from the long list included in the teachings of Harley Swiftdeer Reagan are the Barn Owl, bringer of dreams, who, with his smooth, soundless flight, perfectly symbolises his appointed role; and the Domestic Cat who teaches spiritual patience and relaxation while remaining constantly aware. The American Indians, very conscious of the interdependence of all living things, recognise themselves in the animals and acquire self-knowledge through their close contact with them.

Many religions ascribe animal attributes to their deities. The Hindu god of good fortune, Ganesh, has the head of an elephant and the body of a man, while Vishnu is depicted as a boar. In the hierarchy of being the Hindus give animals equal status with humans.

The need to find animals to symbolise human characteristics has even led to the creation of mythical beasts – the Unicorn, for instance, has appeared in legends, dreams and paintings since medieval times. What does it represent? Freedom, perhaps, and strength, with the single horn a symbol for one-pointed and integrated spiritual power. Some mythical beasts are depicted as part-human and part-animal – the Centaur (horse-man), the Minotaur (bull-man), the Echnida (snake-woman), the Sphinx (woman-lion-bird), the Siren (bird-woman), the Mermaid (woman-fish). Their animal features personify the animal strengths and powers that make up humanity, and enable mankind to draw on them.

Most of the time we are unaware that we are using animals as unconscious projections. They symbolise a part of ourselves with which we may not be in touch, which is beyond our understanding and control; we therefore perceive them as gods. The gods of mythology are essentially hidden aspects of our own humanity, and once they are discovered and faced and integrated within ourselves, they lose their separateness and power over us; some of their power is absorbed into the conscious personality.

Irrational fear of animals might also be explained by this theory: we are really afraid of the part of ourselves symbolised by the animal. Think of the animals of your nightmares. Mine is usually a black fish, very primeval, and even when I see a large black fish in real life, I shiver a little. In consequence animals have suffered for centuries as symbols of the animal aspects of ourselves with which we are ill at ease; we forget that they are beings in their own right, worthy of our respect.

In Ancient Greece and Rome the cat was regarded more as an effective controller of vermin than as a creature to be revered, although its independence was sometimes used by the Romans as a symbol of freedom. In China, however, it was honoured for its aura of self-contained meditation, an attribute highly prized within the Buddhist tradition. The Chinese also understood the feminine aspect of the cat, and considered cats the most suitable pets for women.

The Babylonians believed that their temple cats enshrined the souls of the dead, and a similar belief lingered on amongst the Burmese and Thais well into this century. Some of the temple cats of Thailand bear a 'Temple Mark' – two dark patches towards the lower part of the neck, as if some deity had picked up the cats' original ancestor and left a distinctive hand-print on its fur.

In Muslim countries the cat has always been highly regarded since the time of the Prophet, not as an object of worship but as a companion to be treated with affection and respect. This is because Mohammed had a beloved cat of his own – Muezza – to which he accorded the utmost courtesy and consideration.

In ancient Egypt the cat was originally associated with the great Mother Goddess Isis, but eventually a new cat goddess emerged, named Bast or Bastet. Bast is sometimes referred to as the daughter of Isis and Osiris, but others believe she is a later version of the Mother Goddess.

The domestic cat was especially sacred to Bast who held a central position in Egyptian mythology, being the second member of the Triad of Memphis, and her cult lasted for nearly 2,000 years. Other names for Bast were Oubastis and Pasht, and it is from the former that our words 'puss' and 'pussy' are thought to have derived. Bast was identified with fertility, maternity and pleasure, and enjoyed dance and music. Watching cats play I often feel they are the epitome of dance.

A goddess represents feminine power, and symbolises different aspects of feminine virtues which are universal. Bast's qualities were echoed in other cultures, too. The Greeks called her Artemis, the Romans Diana, the Scandinavians Freya or (Freyia) and the Saxon goddess was Frigga. The cat was associated with all of them, but only in a symbolic sense; living cats never again gained the same respect, care and reverence which they had held in Egypt.

In India the cat-goddess Sasti represents maternity, and as Hindu and Parsee religions advocate respect for all living things it can only be hoped that their cats are treated in a benevolent way, although the cat in India has never held the central place that it assumed in Egyptian mythology.

Throughout history, therefore, the cat has been not only a feminine symbol, but a symbol of the feminine at its most potent. Both Isis and Bast were connected with the moon, and so were regarded as being particularly powerful, since the moon and the sun were such potent and mystical symbols to the Ancient Egyptian mind.

Recognising the symbolic femininity of cats and awed by their ability to see in the dark, the Egyptians used them not only to represent the feminine aspect of Bast, but also her dual nature, embracing both the sun and the moon. Just as the sun was able to see through the gloom of the underworld through which it journeyed at night, so the cat was able to see in the dark. The animal's luminous eyes were believed to mirror the sun's rays when it was otherwise invisible to man, just as the moon reflected the light of the solar orb. Bast, the Cat-moon, during the night held in her eye the sun, and kept watch by using the light he bestowed on her. The ability to see in the dark is very like the ego penetrating the unconscious, and perhaps this quality was symbolic in Bast of a more integrated and balanced personality. The cat reflected this with its cool, self-contained demeanour. One has only to look at the beautiful Egyptian statues of Bast to feel her power.

The goddesses Sekhmet and Bast apparently originated as one deity, and some books describe them as sisters. They certainly seem to represent different aspects of the same persona. Sekhmet, appropriately, was usually depicted as lion-headed, her nature being that of a goddess of war. She needed masculine strength, and the lion represents not only the cat (feminine), but also physical power and strength (masculine).

I do not think it is by chance that the lion has been chosen throughout the ages to be the symbol of tribal chiefs, kings, and even Christ the Son of Man. The lion symbolises the authority of kingship, harmonising both feminine and masculine, ruling both male and female.

Sekhmet is also linked with Hathor, the daughter of Ra. When mankind had so angered Ra that he determined to exact vengeance, he sent Hathor to carry out his will, and it was as Sekhmet that she descended to earth and brought about mankind's near-destruction. This myth is very interesting as it has a clear relevance to our own time. It is rooted in a society perhaps more under the control of the unconscious than the average person living today – hence the relative power of the gods and goddesses in the Ancient Egyptian mind; people would have felt more vulnerable if they were still struggling to build their egos. To the Egyptians the gods seemed so powerful that the idea of making their own decisions and not being dominated by archetypes and instincts would have been very frightening. It would have needed a great struggle to break free from those influences, and the psyche does not easily accept radical change. It will devise all kinds of fears to keep us in a situation – even a negative one – in which it feels secure. Alison, whom I described in Chapter 5, is a vivid example of this.

A god or goddess had to be appeased or something terrible would happen: the crops would fail, or some mysterious disease would strike their children down. Hence the myth of Sekhmet had the effect of keeping the people under control, while also giving them a feeling of reassurance and security. The problem for us as civilised people is that we tend to ignore our unconscious, to suppress and wound the instincts. Yet if these instincts, the archetypes or 'gods', are not accepted as part of the condition for wholeness, we cannot achieve a balanced psyche. In other words, we need to integrate our 'gods' and 'goddesses' into our lives, or sooner or later they will make their presence felt. Sekhmet wreaking vengeance on mankind for displeasing the gods becomes a symbol for all whose lives are disrupted by the backlash of instincts which they have tried to ignore or suppress.

The treatment of the cat in the Christian countries of Europe has not always been respectful or benevolent, and a distrust of the cat is deeply rooted in the Judaeo-Christian tradition. This partly stems from the fact that the cat is only once mentioned in the Bible – and then only in the Apocrypha – and even this is a very negative reference linking the cat with idol-worship. Such an attitude towards the cat is not surprising when one considers how the Jews had suffered at the hands of their Egyptian conquerors. If they associated the cat with the Egyptians, they could hardly be expected to view it impartially; any cat would have been a living reminder of one of the most painful periods in their history.

Yet for the Christian theologians there were still more profound reasons to be suspicious of the cat. As we have seen, in many of the early civilisations the cat was associated with the moon, largely because of its variety of colour and its tendency towards activity during the hours of darkness. Yet in ancient solar rites there also figures the 'Divine Cat of the Sun', and it may be that the origin of the almost universal game of Cat's Cradle was connected with these rites, and with trying to entangle (and thereby control) the Cat of the Sun. It is little wonder that the Christian theologians began to assign a very negative meaning to the cat, and hence to associate it with various forms of ceremonial magic.

Women in Christianity were viewed in a dualistic way. The Christian equivalent of the Mother Goddess, the Virgin Mary, became, not the epitome of female nature but only the personification of womanly virtues; the powerful sensual, sexual, intuitive and independent side of woman was seen as wicked. There is nothing wrong in praising female virtue and symbolising it with the Virgin Mary; what is wrong is to deny the other aspects by saying that they are unnatural and evil. Seeing the powerful feminine qualities as a threat to their authority and self-control, men's solution was to condemn them.

That the Christian Church was also thereby rejecting the unconscious mind is a very real possibility. This would account for the profoundly anti-feminine stance of the early Church, since the unconscious is usually regarded as feminine. It would also help to explain the fanatical opposition of the Church to the Gnostic Churches, whose female priests and prophets must have horrified and deeply disturbed the early Fathers.

In this very narrow Christian perception the unconscious was something to be afraid of: from it arose not only uncontrollable thoughts and feelings that were branded as evil, but also intuition and original thought, which might question the truth and therefore the power of the Church. The desire to suppress and control all these impulses simply diverted more energy to the instincts, and the ensuing mental conflict often led to the infliction of great suffering in the name of piety. Fear is a powerful spur to cruelty, and it was inevitable that innocent women and cats, symbols of men's repressed unconscious, should become victims and scapegoats.

With this in mind it is easy to see why the history of the cat in Christian Europe has been such a chequered one. During the early Middle Ages its skill in catching plague-bearing rats brought it a certain popularity, despite clerical disapproval. In the thirteenth century, however, a campaign of persecution began, largely as a reaction to the revival in the Rhineland of the cult of Freyia, and

during the next four hundred years many thousands of cats needlessly lost their lives.

The attribution of remarkable powers to the cat (however benevolent these powers might be) cannot have helped it, and the less these powers were understood the easier it must have been to succumb to superstitious fear. The Egyptian name for the cat was Mau, meaning a seer, and the Egyptians linked the cat with the all-seeing Eye of Horus. From early Egyptian times the cat was often regarded as being capable of clairvoyance, and there are many well-documented cases of cats showing fear in the presence of ghostly manifestation. There are also numerous accounts of cats showing terror before an earthquake or volcanic eruption. Many cat owners – including the French writer Dumas – attest to telepathic communication between themselves and their cats, and I have already described, in the previous chapter, the cat's proven ability to heal. An animal with such amazing – and beneficial – powers would inevitably come to be regarded sooner or later as a symbol of the free and mysterious process of spiritual thought. To those who embraced this kind of freedom, the cat was seen as a companion on the path of spiritual progress. But to the man or woman of restricted perception and closed mind (perhaps afraid because of a negative unconscious) to whom this freedom was a threat, the cat would appear as a fearful and loathsome creature. When one adds the extra dimension of the cat as a symbol of the feminine element in man's nature, how fearful indeed the cat must have seemed to those early Christians who lacked an understanding of the inner self made possible by modern psychology.

The history of the revering – and persecution – of the cat is thus in many ways a history of how much – or how little – different human societies have valued both the unconscious mind (the mysterious, feminine, intuitive side of our nature) and the mystical, illuminative path of the spiritual quest. Those who feared this quest – that is, feared direct knowledge of the nature of God, the universe and themselves, and preferred to compensate by concentrating on outward ceremonies and structures – naturally also feared the cat. Those who embraced the quest joyfully also took the cat to their hearts, and treated it with affection and respect. As we are now seeing a great upsurge of interest in – and affection for – the cat in our present-day society, may we perhaps deduce from this a new openness to the spiritual quest?

Aniela Jaffé writes about animals as symbols of the instincts in *Man and his Symbols*:

> Suppressed and wounded instincts are the dangers threatening civilised man; uninhibited drives are the dangers threatening primitive man. In both cases the 'animal' is alienated from its true nature; and for both, the acceptance of the animal soul is the condition for wholeness and a fully lived life. Primitive man must tame the animal in himself and make it his helpful companion; civilised man must heal the animal in himself and make it his friend.

In other words, the condition of man's psyche is perhaps the overwhelming prerequisite for a safe environment. It is here that man must take the first steps towards saving the earth from pollution and destruction, for without respect for himself in the fullest sense of the word, he will not respect the earth and its occupants.

In primitive times animals were respected more out of fear than anything else, although man's awareness that he depended on them for many of his material requirements must have been a contributing factor. At this stage of his development he felt overwhelmed by his instincts, lacking a strong enough ego to contain them. He recognised animals as symbols of these instincts, and in his desire to dominate them, he set about their capture and domestication, while sharpening his ability to defend himself against the more aggressive species. In doing so he boosted his self-esteem and sense of superiority, until eventually his ego became predominant.

Today the individual may try to break free of a dominant ego, but society as a whole is largely responsible for our attitude towards each other. Parents can and should teach their children to respect and care for others (by others I am including animals), for although each of us is an individual we are not separate from others. But because we live in a society that believes in the so-called success of the individual, even at the expense of others, we are not encouraged to look outside our small ego-dominated selves to realise that the acceptance of our animal souls – our instincts – is necessary for a condition of wholeness. Animals, as symbols of these instincts, will only be respected and accepted, not suppressed and abused, when man accepts the whole of himself.

If we cannot accept the 'dog' within us we are going to kick the dog in our path. So through the process of acceptance of our animal soul, we are healing not only ourselves but also our relationships with the environment and with all the other forms of life which share it with us.

There is a widely held misconception that a divide exists between man and animals, as though we were beings of a totally different order. We tend to separate creation into 'them' and 'us', and every living being which is not human is regarded as animal and inferior. This gives us an unrealistic view of ourselves in relation to other species; we need to redevelop our link with them and realise that we too are very much animals. For some people this is difficult enough, but I wonder how we shall all consciously and symbolically perceive animals in years to come, now that we are becoming aware that they are not just bundles of instincts, and that some, including cats, are able to formulate theories, have expectations, and are capable of problem-solving.

Certainly our psychology seems closely linked; I am often amused and surprised at the 'humanness' of my cat friends, or should I say the 'catness' of my human friends? With my own cat household, I have noticed that if my male cat is not allowed out, his energies quickly turn to mischief, which includes teasing my female cat. Have you noticed the same with children? Just keep them in and watch!

If I accidentally hurt one of my cats, or if they have to

spend time in a cattery, they will often let me know they are upset by a show of indifference to me – just for a while, and then they make up with a display of affection. A friend tells me that one of her cats will reprimand the other when it has caused its companion concern, for instance by failing to show up at the end of the day when called. Are we so different?

Before you cry, 'But my cat is capable of aggression, and I am not!' consider how little of your unconscious you really know. It is my experience that inside most cat owners there lurks a leopard – and that is not something to be frightened of, but a source of dynamic power to be recognised and channelled in a positive way.

Man claims superiority by reason of his spirituality, but he is more destructive than any other animal. While our fellow creatures for the most part take from life what they need and leave the rest to exist in its own space and time, we destroy anything and everything if we feel it is to our advantage – and this includes other human beings. What price spirituality! There can be no spirituality unless we become whole, and this involves embracing all life. A spiritual path which believes that animals play no part in the process of enlightenment is a *dead end*.

While here in the West we have only just started to explore these concepts, native cultures – for example, the Punan Dyaks of Borneo – believe in a Tree of All Life: man is the tree and in his branches are all the animals and all the races of men, each representing an aspect of self, a perfect symbol. It never ceases to amaze me that such wisdom, which when understood seems so obvious, is not part of our culture, but appears to have been accepted for many years by people we call uncivilised!

One thing is certain: if we live *beside* animals instead of above them, our lives will be greatly enriched; we shall constantly learn from them, not only about their nature, but also about ourselves.

9

What I Have Learnt From My Own Cats

By studying the behaviour of my various cats over the years, I have been able to appreciate the changes that have taken place in my life. My first cat, Whiskey, was my companion through my teenage years. Although in many ways she was an ideal pet, very adept at listening and quiet and gentle, she never really came out of herself.

The years went by, and I gained a little more confidence. A month after I was married I saw my first Siamese. There was no going back – I had to have one! I chose a seal point male, and although I picked the one who was on his own and different from the others, he was also the most mischievous kitten in the litter – at that time I had a lot of energy. I named him Tangi. However, even by then my marriage was unhappy, and I projected strongly onto Tangi. He became very close to me, and as he did not like me to leave the house he contrived all kinds of tricks to detain me. I consulted our local vet, who suggested that another cat would help to keep him occupied, so lessening his reliance on me. At first I was unhappy with the idea: I was dependent on Tangi for love and the thought of having to share him made me a little wary. However, I managed to overcome that, and in due course I acquired Mieling, a chocolate point female Siamese.

For a week Tangi ignored her completely, and I began to think that he might never accept her. He was obviously feeling just like me, but Mieling's funny little face and her courage won us both over, and I soon began to love her too. Tangi represented my male unconscious and Mieling my female conscious, and as the unhappy years of my marriage unfolded, Tangi and Mieling, and later my son Matthew, were my only source of joy. Tangi changed from being very energetic into a subdued and quiet cat as my male energies became more and more suppressed and depressed – I had a very dominant husband. Mieling remained her normal self, although slightly more nervous. After my son was born the cats never harmed him and he never harmed them, but he seemed unable to develop a really close attachment to them: his deep feelings, like mine, had become locked up in the unhappiness of the domestic situation.

Tangi always seemed to have a gentle understanding of my pain, and both cats remained very close to me to the end of their lives. Tangi was 16 when he died and Mieling lived to 18. But my next pair of cats tell a very different story . . .

By the time I acquired Hooli and William I had been divorced just over a year and was dedicated to the study of self-understanding. Mieling had died in October, leaving me very distressed and lonely; I thought a period without cats might be a good idea, partly because I felt I could not bear to face the pain of eventual bereavement again.

By December, however, Matthew and I were already missing cats around the house, and the thought of two young kittens, at a time when life seemed to be opening up and starting anew, was an exciting proposition. Matthew was particularly keen because he had never had a kitten; Tangi and Mieling were already seven years old when he was born. We had also discussed the possibility of having female kittens and mating them. As it was close to Christmas I said the first kitten could be Matthew's present, and he would be allowed to choose one, name it and organise its breeding. One thing we both agreed was that it should be a female Siamese, and a tabby point, either seal or chocolate. So the search began.

After endless telephone calls and looking through newspaper advertisements, I traced two litters in the Plymouth area. The first had chocolate point and chocolate tabby point females. The second had just one red point male left from a litter of three. Not wanting a male, and not having much liking for red points, we felt sure the first litter would have the kitten we wanted and we arranged to go and look them over. The house was full of Siamese, busy climbing curtains, opening drawers, putting paws in cups of coffee and generally being Siamese Cat. The atmosphere was exhilarating!

Matthew watched the kittens and said he quite liked the little chocolate tabby point female, but as it was the first litter we had looked at, we both felt it would be nice to see the other litter after all. So tearing ourselves away from the entertainment, we explained we were going to visit a red point male a mile or so away, but as we didn't want a male, or a red point, we thought we would probably be booking the little female. However, our unconscious had other ideas, as we were soon to discover.

We arrived at the house of the second litter. The three kittens and their mother were in a kitten pen in the lounge. The kitten which was trying to see what was going on, climbing the sides of the pen while his sister and brother slept, was William. I felt an instant attraction – he was wonderful! Let out of his pen, he shot up and down the room with his tail puffed out, playing and leaping for the sheer joy of living. His colour was incredible, a soft peach, and in his blue eyes there was a wonderful sense of humour and mystery.

Matthew and I sat looking at William, absolutely captivated. I was praying that Matthew was feeling the same as me, because the first kitten was going to be his choice, and I felt that I had to keep my promise. I had fallen in love with a red point male kitten, all the things I thought I didn't want! But luckily Matthew felt just the same, and asked if we could have William. It was arranged that we would bring him home in two weeks' time.

We both came home on a high, and I felt so excited I had difficulty sleeping that night. So strong is the pull of your unconscious in feelings of attraction that it can override all your choices made out of reason. William arrived, and we delighted in his sheer zest for life, his sham fights, his sense of fun, and his beauty – he was one of the most playful and intelligent cats I have ever met. He quickly learned to retrieve his favourite toy, a sheepskin ball, which accompanied him everywhere like a beloved teddy bear. Although we enjoyed his attention we knew it would only be fair to him to give him a companion, as he was far too bright to be left alone with no stimulus. Like an intelligent child, he would quickly turn his energies to destructiveness unless he had some kind of entertainment. We would have to choose another kitten.

The next one was to be my choice, and this time it was definitely to be a female so that we could have some kittens. The choice of a female now felt right, as I already had my male element (or animus) fulfilled by William. I started searching for another Siamese, and traced a breeder who had a litter of tabby points due, expressing an interest in any females that came in the litter. Two females were born, and I said I would probably have one of them, but would wait until they were bigger before choosing. This kitten had to be strong and healthy, because I intended mating her.

Meanwhile Matthew, his friend and I visited the National Cat Show at Olympia. Lecia, my friend with the limping cats, also came with us. For many years she has owned both Burmese and Siamese cats, and had tried to explain to me the subtle difference between the two breeds. She hoped that one day I would have a Burmese, as hers had brought her so much pleasure. When we got to the show we walked along the lines of Burmese cats, and I had to admit I found the chocolate ones very attractive.

I decided that one day I would have one, but for the moment, I thought I would still choose a tabby point Siamese.

While waiting for the two little tabby point kittens to grow, Lecia and I visited a breeder of Burmese cats in Somerset. It was here that Lecia was going to board her cat for a month, while she went on holiday. It was a lovely cold, dry January day, and all the way to Somerset we saw rainbows and hawks: I should have known that day was going to be pure magic. When we arrived at Gill's she had a litter of Burmese kittens just about ready to go to their new homes. They were enchanting. As Gill usually had people waiting for kittens, I thought they must all be sold and, feeling quite safe, I said, 'I don't suppose you have a female chocolate kitten, suitable for breeding, and ready to go today, do you, Gill?' I was thinking that even if they weren't all sold the combination of requirements was so difficult to achieve that the possibility of success was remote.

I should have known better. Without hesitating she handed me a chocolate female. What should I do now? I felt strongly pulled to this little kitten, but I had already decided to have a Siamese. I convinced myself that I would be owning three cats after all, and the kitten came back with us, tucked into my coat, another case of the unconscious dictating my choice. She was called Ethereal Bryony, and her mother had been aptly named Magic.

William fell on her with sheer delight – at last another kitten to play with! He acted as if it was a hundred Christmasses all rolled into one. I don't think I shall ever forget the moment when I put her on the floor of the lounge for the first time. They played instantly, and she settled in straight away, showing no sign of homesickness. William allowed her to eat his food, gazing at her the while with sheer adoration. We had intended to name her after a Moon-goddess, but during the next week or two it became clear that a livelier name would be more appropriate. Somehow she became Hooli (short for Hooligan).

Hooli and William seemed to fulfil all our cat needs, and with the cost of their upkeep in mind, I decided that two would be enough for the time being. This was January 1986, and in the late Spring of that year my desire for greater self-understanding led me to Yasmin, a Jungian psychologist. The work we were to do together so closely involved the cats that I came to realise just how much of myself I was projecting onto them. It also became clear that I could be helped towards an understanding of myself by watching the way I treated them. My dreams, too, became vitally important in the process of self-understanding. Frequently these involved Hooli and William, and later Hooli's kittens, which I often dreamt were escaping from me as I frantically tried to round them up. I learnt that when in my dreams I was at last able to let them go without worrying, this would be an indication that I was on my way to a greater freedom for myself.

Looking at the kind of cats I had chosen, I realised what progress I had made since my divorce, and looking back to Whiskey, Tangi and Mieling, I was able to see the stages

I had gone through before. William now represented to me a strong male element (my animus). My unconscious energy was strong and beginning to flow again after many years of being suppressed. I had chosen a cat that represented fun and action: he didn't become subdued as Tangi had been, and the more I allowed my feelings to develop the more William blossomed, although at times he became almost too bossy!

Hooli had a wonderful female energy, with a look that many Burmese have, which seems to say, 'Don't push me too far, or I will get angry.' I have come to love her angry expression, and I know just how she feels. As I started to understand my female consciousness, Hooli also developed her character, while William took a back seat: they were simply reacting to my feelings which I was unconsciously transmitting to them. The objective was to balance this consciousness and energy: while allowing my male unconsciousness the chance to flow, my female consciousness had to exist, and by understanding both they could work in harmony. Matthew had obviously chosen William because as a young teenager he was struggling to fix his own masculine image, and William represented that; so it was fortunate that the image we both needed at that time was the same: mine for my unconscious, Matthew for his conscious.

How I treated the cats was also giving me a good indication of how I was feeling. At the beginning of my course with Yasmin I learnt how you project your fears onto those close to you, and by watching how I treated William and Hooli I gained a fair insight into how I viewed the world. The closer I wrapped them up and tried to protect them, the more negative I was feeling; and the more positive I became the more freedom they experienced. I still watch for this now, and if I find that I am being over-protective, I sit down and try to understand what it is I am worrying about. If only I had realised this with my first two cats, I could have recognised the danger signals as the fences around me grew higher and higher.

When Hooli was one year old she was mated to a very handsome tom cat, and in due course seven kittens were born. This experience was great fun, with William becoming a very attentive uncle, teaching them all to fight and get into mischief, while Hooli watched it all with a knowing look. When it was time for the kittens to leave, like any responsible breeder I took great care to find them suitable homes, and to explain to the new owners the possible dangers the kittens might face. But I still experienced a lot of irrational anxiety, showing me that I had work left to do on myself. My fears that the kittens would not be safe meant I still had negative feelings about myself.

What I must never forget is that although my cats presented these images of myself to me, they are in fact individuals in their own right; they are not *me*.

And although I used them to help me understand myself, I also have to respect them for what they are. Following this process of self-understanding is thus leading me to a richer and fuller life for both myself and my cats.

Conclusion

To round off this book, I want to summarise the importance of your relationship with your cat companion. The words which I feel best express this are response, respect and responsibility.

Your response to your cat, and your ability to accept the image it presents shows your desire to contact your own feelings. When you touch a cat it often responds with a purr, showing pleasure and contentment. You relax with the cat, delighting in its happiness. Your demonstration of love is returned to you by the cat's response: this gives you a feeling of well-being, and I believe the cat also receives a similar benefit.

As children, or as kittens, we all need love to develop properly: it makes us feel good about ourselves, so that we see the world from a more positive viewpoint. Love demonstrated by touch is very important, and our cat companions give us the opportunity to express and experience this. In responding to the cat's needs, whether by love or by attending to its general welfare, we are probably responding to those needs within ourselves.

The same principle applies to respect. Once you have learnt to respect yourself, you find it much easier to respect the needs of all living things. Respect for yourself shows a certain degree of understanding: until you understand your own needs, how can you respect them? This does not mean being selfish: selfishness can be destructive, as it does not take into account your need to love and be loved.

This inevitably leads to responsibility: responsibility for yourself, your cat, and ultimately for planet Earth. If response and respect are lacking, there tends to be no responsibility. When you undertake to look after a cat, you domesticate it, and assume responsibility for its welfare.

Your responsibility to the animal world goes much farther than you may at present realise. By sharing your life with animals you help each other to a greater awareness. American Indians knew that all nature is interdependent, and that in caring for animals you are also caring for yourself both emotionally and physically. The old American Indian saying, that when an animal is made extinct a part of man dies, does not only refer to the ecological balance of the earth, but is also echoed in your psyche.

In a recent television programme I watched a man hang-gliding alongside an eagle – two spirits truly joined in understanding and expressing each other's feelings, with man having the humility to enter the eagle's world. To anyone with an animal companion this is perhaps the greatest gift of all, a joining of spirits in responsiveness and respect for each other's being, able to communicate with the very essence of life shared by both, able to understand the true meaning of Oneness.

Glossary

ANIMA
The personification of the feminine aspect of a man's unconscious.

ANIMUS
The personification of the masculine aspect of a woman's unconscious.

ARCHETYPE
A primordial universal mental image (e.g. Earth Mother, Wise Old Man, etc.) within the collective unconscious, the psychological counterpart of instinct.

THE EGO
The awareness of self, and the centre of the conscious mind.

INSTINCT

An innate impulse
unconsciously determined;
psychological urges that
are perceived by the senses.
Instincts are collective (not
exclusive to one individual).

INSTINCTIVE SYMPATHY

A natural or inherent sharing
of, and being simultaneously
affected by, another being's
conscious or unconscious
feelings, emotions and
thoughts, usually without
being aware that this process
is taking place, or that what
one is experiencing does not
originate from oneself.

JUNGIAN PSYCHOLOGY

The system of therapy
developed by Carl Jung, one
of Sigmund Freud's early
colleagues. Jungian psychology
puts more emphasis on the
central self, and the spiritual
context of life. Those readers
who are interested in Jungian
therapy should contact:
The Society of Analytical
Psychology, 1 Daleham
Gardens, London NW3.

NEUROSIS

A conflict within the unconscious which can lead to irrational behaviour.

PROJECTION

Recognising and identifying with something of yourself in another person or animal, and the projecting of your feelings onto the other person or animal.

THE UNCONSCIOUS

The content of the unconscious includes everything known but not being thought about at the moment, all things known but now forgotten, unnoted sense perceptions, involuntary feelings, thoughts and desires, and all future possibilities. Also in the unconscious are qualities that are not individually acquired, but inherited. These include instincts and archetypes which are universal. All these things within our unconscious are found to affect our behaviour.

Bibliography

There are a number of books about Jung and Jungian psychology. A clear general introduction is:

An Introduction to Jung's Psychology by Frieda Fordham, Penguin Books, Harmondsworth, 1953.

Among the books written or edited by Jung himself, the general reader will find the following accessible and helpful:

Memories, Dreams, Reflections by C. G. Jung, Collins and Routledge & Kegan Paul, London, 1963. (Contains a most useful glossary of Jungian terms.)

Man and his Symbols, edited by C. G. Jung, Aldus Books, London, 1964. (Explains the significance of symbolism in dreams and art.)

I would also recommend:
Animus and Anima by Emma Jung, Spring Publishers, Dallas, 1981.

I have consulted a number of books about cats during the writing of this book, particularly the following:
Incredible Cats: The Secret Powers of Your Pet by David Greene, Methuen, London, 1984.
The Book of the Cat, edited by Michael Wright and Sally Walters, Pan Books, London, 1980.
The Encyclopaedia of the Cat by Angela Sayer, Octopus Books, London, 1979.
Behavior, Development and Training of the Cat: A Primer of Feline Psychology by F. J. Sautter and J. A. Glover, Arco Publishing, New York, 1978.
The Cat in the Mysteries of Religion and Magic by M. Oldfield Howey, Charles E. Tuttle Co., Japan, 1981.
Just So Stories by Rudyard Kipling, Macmillan, London, 1902 (current edition 1989).
Cat Talk: What Your Cat is Trying to Tell You by Carole C. Wilbourn, Macmillan Publishing Co., Inc., New York, 1979; Collier Macmillan Publishers, London.
Alice's Adventures in Wonderland by Lewis Carroll, Macmillan, London, 1865 (current edition 1989).
Through the Looking Glass by Lewis Carroll, Macmillan, London, 1872 (current edition 1989).
Manual of Canine Behaviour, by Valerie O'Farrell, BSAVA Publications, Cheltenham, 1986.
Understanding Your Cat by Michael W. Fox, Coward,

McCann & Geoghegan, New York, 1974; Blond & Briggs Ltd., London.

Those who would like to know more about the native American Indian culture may find useful:
The Medicine Wheel Earth Astrology by Sun Bear, Prentice Hall Inc., Englewood Cliffs, NJ, 1980.

Index